Unfamiliar Paths

Unfamiliar Paths

The Challenge of Recognizing the Work of Christ in Strange Clothing

–A Case Study from France–

David E. Bjork

William Carey Library

P.O. BOX 40129
PASADENA, CALIFORNIA 91114

> The William Carey Library is pleased to present this book with certain features intended to facilitate the interchange of ideas between all other writers who are drawn upon in this book. Chapter numbers are to be found in the running heads on each recto page. References cited at the end of the book include references to the pages on which those references are cited. Notes at the end of each chapter are accompanied by page references to the place they arise in the text of that chapter. In addition, in order to search for any phrase or term in the entire book, a floppy disk version is available separately.

Published by
William Carey Library
P.O. Box 40129
Pasadena, California 91114
(626) 798-0819

"Scripture taken from the HOLY BIBLE, NEW INTERNATIONAL VERSION. Copyright © 1973, 1978, 1984 International Bible Society. Used by permission of Zondervan Bible Publishers."

ISBN 0-87808-278-6

To my children, Marie-Rose and Andrew-David,
and to my wife, Diane

For eighteen years these three people have loved and served each other
and our French neighbors and friends in ways that have inspired me
and reminded me of my own need to grow in Christlikeness. I cannot
imagine learning the lessons detailed in this book without Diane
and our children. For that matter, I cannot imagine doing anything
without them.

"I will lead the blind by ways they have not known,
along unfamiliar paths I will guide them ..."

Isaiah 42:16

Contents

List of Figures

List of Tables

Acknowledgments

I am grateful to the Missionary Church and the leaders of World Partners for allowing me the freedom to explore the possibilities of ministry as I describe it in these pages. It has been my great privilege to serve under Rev. Eugene Ponchot and Rev. Charles Carpenter, Overseas Directors of the Missionary Church. These men struggled with me over the many issues presented in this book. Their response to my personal and ministerial pilgrimage, in both word and deed, was a continual source of inspiration and motivation. Without their faith, courage, and trust in God's leading I would never have been able to persevere through the many times of frustration and discouragement.

This book is also the result of many hours of prayerful research, study and dialogue with the members of the missionary team of World Partners ministering in France. God used that team of men and women to refine and purify my motives and strengthen my resolve.

Through the years I have had the opportunity to "compare notes" with other evangelical Protestant missionaries ministering in Western Europe. I have also had the privilege of studying under and brushing shoulders with missionary thinkers at Fuller Theological Seminary School of World Mission. These individuals have been a tremendous encouragement and stimulus to me as I have wrestled with the ins and outs of ministry in post-Christendom France.

Today I am blessed to be able to continue to explore the questions raised in the following pages under the supervision of Servant of Servants Foundation. A missionary could not desire to serve under a more courageous and caring board. My wife and I continually thank our Heavenly Father for these men and women, and for the many other people and churches who have continuously supported us by their prayers and financial gifts in our ministry to the French.

My own parents have been a continual source of encouragement and support. They have sought not only to understand the implications of my approach to ministry, but to apply to their situation in Southern California the lessons that I have learned in France.

In reading this book you will sense how important the home is in the kind of ministry that I will describe. Since we have determined that presenting Christ to the French cannot be a set of activities that we do, but rather a way of living, each of the members of my family has been intimately and actively involved in the process outlined in these pages. I am happy to dedicate this book to my children, Marie-Rose and Andrew-David, and to my wife, Diane.

I offer a special thanks to my friends at the U.S. Center for World Mission for encouraging me to write this book, especially to Dr. Ralph Winter. I also thank Roberta Winter, Corinne Armstrong, Lois Baker, Jeanne Lyman, Lisa Sells, and Peggy Sorden for proofreading the manuscript, making helpful comments on it, and entering corrections. Thanks also goes to Kent and Melissa Lawson and Pete Sorden for their work on the cover and graphics. Finally, I am very grateful to David Shaver and the staff at William Carey Library for their willingness to publish this book.

May God richly bless all who read this book and enable it to serve whatever purposes He has in mind for it.

Foreword

Jeffrey Gros, FSC

This volume should be deeply disturbing for anyone who places Jesus Christ at the center of their life and sees the bringing of His good news to the whole inhabited earth as essential to the Church's mission. This book should call all who have given their life to the mission of the Church or who see evangelism as a priority in the Gospel, into a deeper reflection on how one is to live a spirituality of mission and to respond in obedient discipleship in a changing and multicultural society.

While the book is about missionary work in France, in particular, it is finally about how we transcend our own cultural experience to incarnate the Gospel of Jesus Christ in a world where an established Christendom is a thing of the past. Let the U.S. reader, Evangelical or Catholic, not feel too complacent that this volume only touches an ancient, European Christendom culture. One has only to reflect on how both Evangelicalism and Catholicism have become "at ease in Zion" in an American culture whose rhetoric may have Christian overtones, where there is no persecution, but where it is "easy" to be Christian, with or without the passion of the original Gospel of Jesus Christ.

Readers will not agree with the author on many points, undoubtedly, but they will be engaged in an important rethinking of mission at this moment of history. While this volume is targeted at the Evangelical missiologist, it may be more urgent reading by the Orthodox and Catholic leadership, as all Christians mobilize for mission in the increasingly diverse cultural situations of our various mission fields.

As Pope John Paul has continually recalled in his pressing of the New Evangelization, there is no place on earth that is not a mission field. He is especially emphatic in calling Christians—preferably together—in Eastern Europe, Latin America and secularized Western Europe to this renewed task of preaching the Gospel to the nominal

Christian with new vigor, new methods and new commitment to collaboration. I look forward to the day when this volume will be translated into Spanish, Greek, Portuguese and the Slavic languages.

When I was teaching history of Christian thought at Memphis Theological Seminary, a student came up to me and said he could not continue in my course because he was "Pentecostal and fundamentalist," and I was a Roman Catholic. He said this without ostensible bigotry.

From that time forward I always introduced myself as a "Bible-believing Christian in the Roman Catholic tradition." I uncovered for the students the riches of Luther, Augustine, Aquinas and Chrysostom, beginning with their biblical commentaries, rather than their contributions to the maintenance of the orthodox Christian tradition.

Likewise, it was essential for the students from this Evangelical ethos to understand the church planting strategies of the 4th through the 12th centuries and the effective means of evangelism: the monasteries, the creeds and the system of bishops in Europe, North Africa and the Middle East. Yes, "evangelism" includes helping those who read the Bible selectively to understand the "whole" revelation of God in Jesus Christ as transmitted through the Word of God, including the biblical doctrine of the Church and its unity, the Lord's Supper and Baptism, as taught by Paul and the Gospels.

As undergraduates in the 1950s, before the Roman Catholic Vatican Council II (1962-1965), we learned about the "post-Christendom" challenge to the Gospel in France through books like *France Pagan* and *France Alive*, and the pastoral letters of Cardinal Suhard. We were excited by the small group Bible studies, based on a method of observing the secularization of society, judging the situation of the Church and the world in the light of biblical teaching, and acting to bring the Gospel to the nominal Christian and to social relationships. We saw the advantages of a more biblical worship, in the language of the people, with greater participation of the laity—from secularized France. From the evangelical response of creative Catholic leaders, we learned the reforms that would be the dominant themes of our lives in the 60s-90s.

While many of the French "priest workers" and other urban evangelists have had as much difficulty, and as modest success as David Bjork recounted here in this volume, the struggle with the Church's appropriate mission strategy energized a generation of students, and continues to energize missionary Catholics to deepen and adapt post-Christendom modes of evangelizing and discipling modern people into the Christian life.

As a member of a community (De La Salle Christian Brothers) founded in France in 1680 to evangelize the poor, recalling the various waves of evangelical renewal "under the nose" of the established Christendom of the period, we were also nourished on the evangelical option for the poor, resistance to the clerical establishment—baroque in the days of our founder, John Baptist De La Salle, and comfortable middle class Catholicism of mid-century America—and Gospel content in our teaching over against institutional formalism. As with John Wesley, David Bjork and Lesslie Newbigin, so French reformers like De La Salle, Vincent De Paul and a host of founders of women's and men's religious communities in the 19th century have struggled to find a place for an evangelical voice in the midst of a comfortable, and somewhat unconverted, church life.

Of course, in grassroots contexts across the United States, Catholic and Evangelicals marry in Christ, join in outreach to the unchurched together, collaborate in prolife and racial justice activity, pray together in charismatic prayer groups, share faith in Bible studies, and seek to deepen the religious literacy of the Christian people through collaboration on educational programs. Institutions in both communities have been slower to lead this reconciling imperative of Christ, as Bjork documents for the Missionary Church and the Catholic bishop in France, cited in his Appendix.

However, there have been pioneering ventures, like David Hubbard and John Stott's leadership in the Evangelical–Roman Catholic Dialogue on Mission, the Pentecostal–Catholic Dialogue initiated by David Du Plessis, and the Catholic dialogues with the Baptists, in the U.S. with the Southern Baptists and internationally with the Baptist World Alliance. All of these results have important implications for a biblical doctrine of mission and a strategy for inculcating the Gospel in our day.

These dialogues are by no means the most significant theological work to go on between the Catholic Church and Protestants, but they touch on the significant theological concerns of the Evangelical community, and focus more directly on the question of mission. They are not yet adequately known in either Evangelical or Catholic communities. These reports are inescapable resources for any missionary going to serve in a Catholic context, and should be part of the seminary curriculum in all Catholic ministry training programs.

The continuing work of the World Evangelical Fellowship, in dialogues with the Catholic Church, is just a beginning. The mission sending agencies of the Catholic Church and of Evangelical churches and parachurch movements need to find ways of deepening these discussions on collaboration and mission strategy. National and local associations of Evangelicals need to find ways of helping their members into collaboration and conversation with Catholics.

The Gospel and the Kingdom, indeed, provide the imperative for Christians to deal honestly and collaboratively with each other. The word ecumenism still carries negative connotations in many Evangelical circles. Part of our penetration of the Bible is to learn that, indeed, the word ecumenism comes from the Scripture itself (Matthew 28) and its content is integral to the Gospel (John 17). If we are to preach the Gospel, we must have the spiritual discipline to overcome our prejudices, to listen to what God is saying in one another, and to be willing to come under the judgment of the Holy Spirit as we serve His mission.

If we follow Jesus Christ, we follow Unfamiliar Paths, but we also are firmly grounded in the assurance of the Holy Spirit as the final impulse for mission. If this volume helps us to reflect more seriously on the Gospel of Jesus Christ, and our imperative in its service, then we have begun an important step on that path, a path which we trust will lead us to that goal which Christ has laid out for us as the end of history.

Brother Jeffrey Gros, FSC
Associate Director
Secretariat for Ecumenical and Interreligious Affairs
National Conference of Catholic Bishops

Foreword

Ralph D. Winter

Jeffrey Gros in his foreword observes that this book may be disturbing to both Protestant and Catholic. I would add that the effect may very well also be growing and stretching.

Basically, it provides honest and valid insight into the difficulty and the promise of people of faith recognizing the validity of faith in a quite different cultural tradition. As such, its significance reaches far beyond the specific clash of Protestant and Catholic. It will, of course, be highly valuable for all who are struggling with that particular divergence. But it is in powerful ways a case study that is equivalent to the Jew/Greek polarization presented so dramatically in the Christian "New Testament." It reflects and extends those pristine events into a paradigm which can and must be understood as the faith moves out into even more divergent cultural traditions.

Across the centuries as the Judaic scriptures embodying a potent faith spilled over into the languages of major, drastically divergent cultural basins, it has usually taken on forms, ultimately, so different from the source culture that the new forms have usually been regarded by almost everyone as inherently different. Right in Romans 14 Paul struggles to defend a Jewish way of following Christ to Greek followers. Furthermore, with the hindsight of the last 2,000 years we understand that every single one of these resulting various cultural streams of faith, including the Jewish, are extensively particular, odd to outsiders, but also desperately defective in some ways as well as immensely strong and redemptive in other ways.

This stubborn combination of the particular, the defective, and the strong, then, gives rise to the persistent phenomenon in which the adherents of one stream can both denounce other streams legitimately while upholding their own legitimately. Less likely, but also true, some within each tradition can legitimately reject their own while insisting on only the good in another.

Thus, ambiguity is rife, crying out for sensitive clarification. We have seen for centuries how easily and yet how logically one can praise the best in his own society and compare it with the worst in the other. I recall from the time of my own youth hearing a professor point out how curious it is that Protestants and Catholics have tended, in each case, to suspect that the other is "soft on sin." The Protestant says "the Catholic does not need to worry because he merely confesses his sins to the priest," while the Catholic can easily observe, "The Protestant does not even need to confess his sins!"

For too long the Greek stream has decried the Jewish, Latin has decried Greek, German has decried Latin, "Evangelical" has decried the culture of the established state churches of Europe. Quite a few Christians today still look upon the amazing Jewish diaspora at the time of Paul as an inert or erroneous bloc, while in fact it was a tradition of living faith or it would not have attracted hundreds of thousands of *God-fearers* and *devout persons.* It was also legalistic, as religio-cultural traditions usually are.

Quite a few Protestants today look upon the amazing Roman Catholic tradition as an inert or erroneous bloc, whereas it is, like Protestantism itself, both a living faith and a legalistic cultural tradition.

But we have arrived at a time when all such superficial comparisons are out of date. It is not as though criticisms between the streams of faith are no longer in order. In fact, it is now both possible and highly urgent for these streams to learn from each other—from new insight that may involve both keen criticism and wholehearted affirmation. Certainly American Christianity has volumes to learn—even about the meaning of the Bible—from the newer Christian streams in the so-called mission lands with their mind boggling differences. This is especially urgent for an elusive reason.

It is no secret that both Jew and Greek had been exposed to the Biblical Revelation. It is precisely the Bible of Greek speaking Jews which was the foundation on which Hellenic faith was built. Paul realized the all-too-common poverty of both traditions—as well as their legitimacy. He said he was very proud of a Gospel which was the saving power of God for *both* Jew and Greek. Yet, within each of the resulting communities of faith even the most earnest believers had a hard time acknowledging the potential poverty in their own midst or the legitimacy within the other. Paul, as a bicultural person, was probably one of a relatively small group who enthusiastically welcomed the Biblical faith in both sets of clothing.

In actual fact, then, it is safe to say that the majority of even the "true believers" within each stream found it difficult if not impossible to accept those of the other, often antagonistic, cultural tradition, often made worse by political and military opposition. However, Paul's record of genuine, uncompromising recognition of true faith in two radically different cultures (Semitic and Hellenic) stands as a powerful symbol for all time and also an unrelenting measure of the true insight we have into our own faith.

So here is the special reason: in so far as we confuse our faith with our particular culture we may miss the meaning of our faith. And this is where the global, multicultural Biblical faith is seen to be crucially interdependent, like a body, where one part cannot say, "I have no need of you." Precisely where differences may seem to be a puzzling nuisance lies gold to be mined that will enable us to rise above our own culture to embrace the full reality of the Bible and the Christ event as seen from many different angles.

It is so easy to assume that missionaries "take" the faith to those who have nothing. But the Bible constantly refers to earnest souls outside of the Judaic stream of revelation whose "integrity of heart" prepared them for greater insight, and whose character in many cases equalled or exceeded that of the messenger of Abrahamic faith. Indeed Abraham was himself corrected by Abimelech.

Only by giving in a bit concerning our perception of our own cultural monopoly on Biblical faith can we be more fully utilized in the work of the God of all nations, Who, one day, will welcome every tribe and tongue and nation and people—whether or not they follow the same set of rituals!

> Ralph D. Winter
> General Director
> Frontier Mission Fellowship

Chapter 1

When Obedience Leads Us
into the Unknown

"No way," I thought. "There is no way that I am going to go with Marc and Henri to church!"

What a weird situation! Under normal circumstances I wouldn't have thought twice about accompanying my young friends to church. After all, I have attended church services all of my life. But that spring day in 1981 was different. On that day the thought of going with these guys gave me knots in my stomach. No, I really didn't want to go.

At first glance the situation really seems ironic. I was reared in a conservative, "Bible-believing," evangelical [1] Protestant home. And, for as long as I can remember, I was present at church whenever its doors were open. Even during my teen years I found my sense of identity and purpose in my church relationships. Moreover, at a Christian youth camp I had responded positively when I sensed God calling me to a life of missionary service. It was obedience to that missionary call that brought me to my crisis in 1981.

New Horizons

Two years earlier, the Missionary Church (the Christian denomination that we had grown up in) had asked my wife and me to open a new missionary work for them in Europe. So, after a time of prayerful consideration, we moved with our four-year-old daughter and two-year-old son to the Normandy region of northwest France to begin a "church-planting ministry."

After settling in an apartment in a city of about 100,000 people, I began a small Bible discussion group with some students at the local university. What an interesting group of young men that was! If you were to have asked them to identify themselves, the majority of them would have said something like this: "I am French. I am Catholic. I believe in reincarnation. I am an atheist. I am a scientist. I go to a healer when I am sick. I am a rationalist."

As you can no doubt imagine, we had some very engaging discussions as we looked at the life and words of Jesus as recorded in the Gospel of John. Only one or two of these young men claimed to have ever opened a Bible before in their life. Only one of them was a regular attendee in his local Catholic parish church. None of them had ever before investigated the gospel account in this kind of environment.

Over a period of several months we met and slowly progressed through the Gospel. It was exciting to watch each week as these men grappled with the fantastic claims of Jesus of Nazareth. One evening, after our study, Marc and Henri approached me with the request that I accompany them to church the following Sunday.

So here I was faced with a dilemma. These university students were just beginning to come to grips with the person and teachings of Jesus. Their new discoveries had apparently sparked in them a desire to worship. Consequently, they wanted to go to church for the first time since they were children. The only problem was that I had not yet begun the church that I had been sent to France to "start." Besides, Marc and Henri didn't want just to go to a church; they wanted to go to *their* church. These guys had been faithfully attending my study and now they were looking to me for reassurance and guidance. Hesitantly, reluctantly (even fearfully perhaps), I gave in to their urgings.

A Painful Discovery

I will never forget the mixed emotions that I felt when I first entered l'Église St. Pierre. Although I had previously visited several cathedrals and church buildings in France, I had never attended Mass and didn't really know what to expect.

The first thing that struck me was the large number of people present at the Mass. The church was packed with between 600 and 650 people. This was unheard of in our area! In fact, I was later informed that just three years earlier only around 50 people regularly attended

Mass in this same parish. Here, to my amazement, was a full church service.

I also felt very uncomfortable in the liturgical setting. It was a completely foreign environment to me, and I never knew when I was to sit or stand (it seemed that the Catholics were continually changing their position) or when to speak or be silent. I had a difficult time following along in the Missal, and couldn't even join in reciting the Lord's Prayer (this was not something that I had memorized in French). I felt like a fish out of water.

As real as this discomfort was, it was insignificant compared to the devastating experience that took place in the middle of Mass. What occurred hit me so powerfully that I began to tremble. We were standing in prayer when suddenly, unexpectedly, I began to sense the presence of God's Spirit. What I was sensing couldn't be true! *God was not supposed to be there!* Everything that I had been taught, everything that I had taught others said that God would not be present at a Roman Catholic Mass! In other words, I believed that God could go to Mass to convict people of their sinfulness and need of the Savior, but He wouldn't hang around afterwards! My theological convictions were that God's Spirit should not be at a Roman Catholic Mass.

When we left Mass I told my wife, "I am never going to go to Mass again! I don't like what I felt in there!"

Checking It Out

A couple of weeks later another member of our Bible study group "took me by the hand" and led me back to Mass at St. Peter's. Once again I was overwhelmed during the Mass by a sense of God's presence. I imagine that what I felt must have been similar to the emotions Peter experienced when the Holy Spirit fell on Cornelius and his household *before* he had a chance to finish his sermon (Acts 10:44). Peter must have wondered how God could be so quick to give His Spirit to this Roman. This soldier. Peter hadn't had the time to "straighten him out." The Scriptures don't even indicate that Cornelius had time to "repent" and be "converted" (although I am sure that this actually took place). As had happened with Peter in his relationship to Cornelius, God sneaked up on me and surprised me by His grace to an "outsider."

Now, I should remind you that I come from a conservative evangelical Protestant background. I have been taught not to put my trust in what I feel or sense. So when the conflict came between what I was "sensing" and what I "knew to be true," I automatically favored the discernment of my mind. At the same time, in my spirit I was deeply troubled. At the end of the second experience of the Mass I felt led to get together with the parish priest to see if I couldn't sort some of these things out.

We met in Father Norbert's office the following afternoon. During the three or four hours together I shared with him the story that you have just finished reading. He graciously listened, and then shared his own testimony with me. After I had asked him some specific questions concerning doctrines over which our churches are in disagreement, we spent some time in prayer.

This meeting with Father Norbert only deepened my confusion. I continued to sense that I was in the presence of a man in whom dwelt the Spirit of the living God. As I listened to his testimony I could identify specific moments of conversion in his life, and his devotion to our Lord Jesus Christ came through loud and clear. At the same time, he held beliefs that I couldn't accept. How could this be? Was I reading him correctly? At times I felt that we were saying the same things, and at others I sensed that we were in completely different worlds.

In order to try to discern more clearly what was going on, I asked if Father Norbert would meet with me for prayer once a week. As a result we met and prayed together nearly every Wednesday morning for three and a half years. Sometimes we prayed together for 15 or 20 minutes; sometimes this time of sharing and prayer took the entire morning.

I am sad to have to admit that it took three and a half years for God to overcome my religious prejudices. The first hurdle was recognizing Father Norbert as my brother in Christ. That hurdle was overcome rather quickly. As I got to know Father Norbert, as I witnessed the vitality of his faith and the consistency of his obedient submission to the Spirit and the Scriptures, I was not only convinced of his relationship with the Savior, but also challenged in my own walk with Christ. The second hurdle was more difficult to overcome. I was still plagued by the question: How can Father Norbert be an obedient disciple of Jesus Christ and remain a practicing Roman Catholic priest? The words of Paul Billheimer, a former radio pastor and Bible college president, helped me to understand that this is a question between Father Norbert and *God*, and not a question between Father Norbert and *me*:

> If you are scripturally born again you are a member of the Body
> of Christ and a son of my very own Father. As a member of the

same family, you are my own brother, whether you realize it or acknowledge it or not. As far as I am concerned, this is true whether you are a Charismatic or anti-Charismatic; whether you believe that everyone should speak in tongues or whether you believe that speaking in tongues is of the devil; whether you believe that the gifts of the Spirit are in operation in the Church today or whether you believe they ceased at the close of the Apostolic age; whether you are an Arminian and believe in eternal security or in falling from grace; whether you accept only the "King James" or prefer a modern version; whether you believe in baptismal regeneration or no ordinances at all; whether you believe in immersion or sprinkling, infant or adult baptism; whether you wash feet or don't; whether you are a Methodist, Baptist, Presbyterian, Disciples of Christ, Church of Christ, Mennonite, Amish, Seventh Day Adventist, Episcopalian, Catholic ... or no denomination at all; whether you believe in female or only male ordination; whether you think that Saturday is the true Sabbath and should be kept holy or whether you think that the day is indifferent; whether you eat meat or are a vegetarian; whether you drink coffee, tea and soft drinks or only water, fruit juices and milk; whether you wear a toupee or sport a bald head; whether you color your hair or not; whether you are a pre-, a post-, or an amillennialist; whether you are a Republican, a Democrat or a Socialist; whether your skin is white, black, red, brown or yellow; and if there be any other doubtful matters ... over which we differ ... if you are born again, we are still members of the same family and organic parts of the same spiritual Body. *I may think some of your beliefs are as crazy as a loon, but if I have sufficient love for God, agape love, I will not reject you as a person.* (1981:114; *emphasis mine*)

As I got to know Father Norbert I began to realize that God's family extends beyond the limits of my own church denomination and reaches even into unexpected places. Perhaps Jesus was alluding to this reality when he said: "I have other sheep that are not of this sheep pen. I must bring them also. They too will listen to my voice, and there shall be one flock and one shepherd" (John 10:16). I learned through a slow, painful, and drawn-out process that my ability to fellowship with Father Norbert could not be based on shared theological understandings, liturgical practices, or on concepts and opinions concerning "non-essentials." If we were to come together it would have to be on agreement over evangelical truths which are basic to salvation and on our common life in Christ.

Increased Puzzlement

When God broke into my world and showed me that He has sons and daughters in the Roman Catholic Church in France, it was as though He had set off a bomb in my life. Up to that point my church-planting mission in France made sense. As long as I could assume either that the church did not exist in France, or that if it did exist, it was so weakened and compromised by its history that it should be replaced, my mission was clear. Now, however, God had brought me to a different appraisal of the situation.

This new understanding of the contemporary spiritual scene in France raised a whole new set of questions that needed to be addressed as I reformulated my understanding of my missionary task. For example: Is it really necessary for me to establish a "new church" in France? How seriously should I take the faith and witness of the ancient Church in this land? What would be my most appropriate response, as the cultural "outsider" and "guest" in France, to the spiritual needs of the French? What was I supposed to do with these Christian brothers and sisters? Should I ignore them or just pray for them? What sort of relationship was God leading me to establish with them?

One of the important biblical texts that God impressed on me is found in the seventeenth chapter of John's Gospel. I began to wonder if I could effectively witness for Christ in France if I ignored what Francis Schaeffer had called "the final apologetic" (1970:138). Jesus spoke of it in John 17:21, 23 while He was praying for His disciples. He asked the Father:

> That all of them may be one, Father, just as you are in me and I am in you. May they also be in us so that the world may believe that you have sent me ... I in them and you in me. May they be brought to complete unity to let the world know that you sent me and have loved them even as you have loved me.

Because of the prayer of Jesus recorded in this section of Scripture, I felt that I had to be careful not to be divisive in the way in which I ministered.

A second text of Scripture that God used to form my thinking at this juncture is found in Paul's letter to the Philippians. In chapter 2, verses 3 and 4 we read: "Do nothing out of selfish ambition or vain conceit, but in humility consider others better than yourselves. Each of you should look not only to your own interests, but also to the interests of others." In the following verses Paul explains how Jesus

Christ put aside His own divine rights and prerogatives so as to bring us salvation.

The teaching of these two texts, coupled with my own missionary experience in the French Catholic world, has brought me to grapple with some other very important questions: How can I minister in France in such a way that I do not create unnecessary barriers between members of God's household? What are some of the "rights" and "privileges" that God might be calling me, as an evangelical Protestant missionary, to abandon so as to serve Him obediently in France? Recognizing that through my evangelical Christian heritage God has given me a unique set of skills, understandings and convictions, how can I best use them to serve His work in France? Is it legitimate to attempt to lead French men and women to Christ in a way that reinforces their appreciation of their own Christian heritage? Is it possible to form a community of believers in a locale, in which our individual converts find spiritual nourishment and encouragement, without institutionalizing that community (so that the members of that community can remain members of institutional churches and work for renewal within those churches)? To what extent is our pursuit of interpersonal unity with individual Catholic believers enhanced or hampered by organizational unity with the Catholic church (or lack thereof)?

In the chapters that follow, my intention is to propose some answers to these questions. My observations come from my understanding of Scripture and from many years of experience ministering in the French Catholic world.

An Overview of This Book

In the next chapter I look at whether or not we should consider France to be a "Christian country." I argue that although Western civilization in Europe and America is the direct successor and heir of Christendom, we would be naive to believe that the inhabitants of these lands have embraced the person and precepts of Jesus of Nazareth and pledged Him their allegiance.

In chapter 3 I examine some aspects of contemporary French culture. As we look at those attributes that make our task of announcing the gospel message so difficult, I explain why I believe that the situation is not hopeless. It is my purpose in those pages to demonstrate some of the ways in which we Protestant evangelical missionaries can keep from setting our evangelical traditions above Scripture. I plead in favor of not allowing the place we give to our denominational and historical baggage to take precedence over the extension of God's kingdom through evangelistic outreach.

In chapter 4 I examine briefly the history of evangelical Protestant missions in France since the end of World War II. Based on that historical overview, I suggest some ways in which evangelical Protestant missionaries can make adjustments in their ministries which I feel are appropriate and necessary. I argue that if these kinds of change are not made, then we will continue to work against the grain of European history in the twentieth and twenty-first century.

In chapter 5 I demonstrate why I believe that the problems confronting evangelical Protestant missionaries in France will not be resolved by finding new and better methods for the propagation of Christ's message. I argue that the answer to the evangelization of the French does not lie in the implementation of more dynamic, seeker-friendly, North American evangelical forms of worship. I explain why my missionary experience leads me to believe that the realities of ministry in post-Christendom France call us to re-examine the foundational premises of our missional paradigm and the activity orientation of our approach.

In chapter 6 I call for a re-examination of missionary spirituality. It is my conviction that it is our spirituality, not our sociology or anthropology, that should give birth to and establish the limits of our ministry. Without the proper spirituality our ministry might reflect a correct understanding of the dynamics of human interaction in society, but it will not display an appropriate understanding of how God has drawn near to mankind.

In chapter 7 I explain the ways in which I have introduced French men and women to Jesus Christ. In those pages I demonstrate that it is possible to give birth to communities of faith in France that are characterized by New Testament life and vitality. I also explain some of the ways that we have allowed the spiritual, cultural and historical realities that we deal with in this book to shape our approach to ministry in France. This is the place where I describe some of the concrete ways in which I have structured my ministry.

In chapter 8 I examine how it is possible for the followers of Christ to live together in the unity of the Spirit, keeping the bond of peace, even when they don't agree. I demonstrate that there has been a good deal of rapprochement between evangelical Protestants and Roman Catholics in recent years, and that we can and should learn from and with each other. I argue that evangelical Protestant missionaries should function more as heralds than as prophets in their ministry in post-Christendom France.

In the ninth and final chapter of this book I examine the questions: Can there be "one out of many" in the followers of Jesus of Nazareth today? Is the unity for which Jesus prayed only wishful thinking? If it is true that in Christ the old divisions of race and gender and even religion have been abolished (Rom. 10:12; 1 Cor. 7:19; Gal. 3:28; Col. 3:11) and if it is true that there is "one body and one Spirit ... one Lord, one faith, one baptism; one God and Father of all, who is over all and through all and in all" (Eph. 4:4-6), then how can we make our unity visible? Drawing from the example of the divine Trinity, I propose that unity with other believers, like love between people, is not a static state to be achieved. Neither is it a product to be produced! Rather, the Trinity reminds us that the process *is* the product.

Concluding Thoughts

In Isaiah 42:16 we read God's words to His servant:

> I will lead the blind by ways they have not known,
> along unfamiliar paths I will guide them;
> I will turn the darkness into light before them
> and make the rough places smooth.
> These are the things I will do;
> I will not forsake them.

How difficult it is for us to walk along unfamiliar paths! The inner struggles of such an experience become even more apparent when we add the fact that we are blind to where these paths might be leading us.

When we began our missionary work in France in 1979, we did not imagine that it would look the way it does today. We thought that it would be similar to what we had already experienced. We assumed that God would lead us along a more familiar trail. Instead, God has led us into situations where we have felt very uncomfortable. He has forced us to open our eyes to realities that we did not want to face. He has taught us that even if, after eighteen years of ministry in France, we don't have definitive answers to give to the questions listed above, that's okay. Sometimes in our desire to arrive at our destination we forget that in God's view the trip is at least as important as the arrival. In other words, God seems to be just as interested in our walk of faith as He is in our arriving at the "right" understandings.

While I acknowledge that I lack the final answers to many of these questions, my experience as an evangelist, disciple maker, and church-planter in Europe has convinced me that if we don't approach these issues in new ways, the spread of the gospel will be hampered. I am increasingly convinced that the kingdom of God will not expand significantly around the world as a result of our simply doing in a bigger or better way what we have always done. Ministry in the name of Jesus Christ, in countries such as France, presents the missionary community with challenges and opportunities that call into question the most widely accepted of our missional paradigms [2] and many of our methodologies.

Through the years my wife and I have watched as God has stripped us of many of our presuppositions, convinced us of our ignorance, and persuaded us to step out into the unknown in our ministry to the French. I hope that as you read the following pages you will sense some of the conflicts and fears, as well as some of the joys and blessings that we have encountered as God has led us into the unfamiliar surroundings of the Roman Catholic world. I pray that the story of our pilgrimage will encourage you to step out by faith into the unknown territory where God wants to lead you.

Notes

1. (p. 1) I agree with Donald Bloesch that the word *evangelical* "signifies an emphasis within Christendom or historic Christianity, one that intends to include as well as exclude. Its specific reference is to the doctrinal content of the gospel itself, with the focus on the vicarious, atoning sacrifice of Christ, on the unsurpassable grace of God revealed in Christ, which is laid hold of not by works of the law but by faith alone (Rom. 3:21-28; Col. 2:11-14; Eph. 2:4-8). All Christianity will contain an evangelical element; otherwise the very claim to be Christian would be suspect" (1983:3-4).

2. (p. 10) Philip Butin states that within the various academic disciplines where it is used, the term *paradigm* often refers to "a comprehensive, organizing pattern of thought that becomes exemplary or controlling for the ongoing work of an individual scholar or a scholarly com-munity. It may also be used less technically to refer to any important example, pattern, or model that governs or consistently informs a set of ideas, relationships, or interactions" (1994:133). It is in this latter sense that I employ it in this book.

Chapter 2

"I Am French, I Am Catholic, I Am an Atheist!"

From time to time as I present my ministry in evangelical circles in the United States, I am shocked to hear people talk as if France is not a legitimate mission field, that it is somehow Christian and therefore off limits to missionaries. Twenty years ago this way of thinking would not have surprised me at all. Twenty years ago I too considered France to be a "Christian country" like the United States or Canada.

I used to feel that France (along with other Western lands) is not as legitimate a target for missional reflection and activity as are other parts of the world. In fact, I first went to France simply to study French. My goal at that time was to learn the language in order to prepare myself for missionary service in Haiti. Before immersing myself in contemporary French culture, I too believed that Christian missional reflection and activities should focus first and foremost on the emerging nations, on the poor, and on the unreached peoples of the world, like the Muslims, the Hindus and the Buddhists.

Don't misunderstand me; I continue to agree that the unreached peoples of the world found in these three blocs of humanity present a formidable challenge for Christian missions. However, I have also come to realize that the majority of people living in post-Christendom lands also resist our message. Today I oppose the idea that it is somehow more important or necessary that missiologists focus their attention on those peoples located outside the scope of historic Christendom. I contend that the love of God for all the peoples of the world compels us to look *also* on the spiritual condition of Western Europe with missional eyes. For, although these peoples are located outside the "10/40 Window," I think that we are either naive or deceived if we consider them second-rate candidates for missional reflection and activity. Moreover, I have found that many of the fundamental questions pertaining to the communication of the gospel and the expansion of the kingdom of God are the same regardless of where one finds oneself.

I agree with those missiologists who affirm that the masses of humanity found in Western Europe cannot be classified among the unreached peoples of our planet. They were among the first to *hear* the gospel. And they were among the first to *embrace* Christianity. However, we should remember that they were also among the first to *reject* Christianity. Furthermore, the history of the last few decades of missional activity in Western Europe tells us that the contemporary missionary methods used to present Christ to unreached peoples have proven ineffective on these resistant peoples. In spite of all this, few missiologists have made these populations the object of their reflection. [1]

Have We Been Tricked by Our Language?

You might be surprised that I refer to a "Christian country" like France as "resistant" to Christianity. Perhaps you are wondering how I can assert that the French must be approached missionally at the same time that some thinkers consider France to be "one of the most Christian countries in the world." Are these missiologists and I looking at the same country? If we are considering the same data, how can our conclusions be so contradictory? These questions are of the utmost importance and merit our reflection.

Language and Meaning

Some of the confusion about whether or not Western European peoples are "Christian" peoples stems from the slippery nature of language and the relationship between words and the ideas that are assigned to them. One element of this is the common and persistent myth about language: that it is a part of the nature of words to contain their meanings (Kraft 1991:33). According to this erroneous view, the word "Christian" contains its own meaning upon which everyone should agree. The problem with this understanding is that the word "Christian," like many other important words, has different meanings to different groups of people. Contemporary linguists inform us that, rather than words containing their own meanings, the meaning of words is determined from the way they are used (Black 1995:123). Unfortunately, the word "Christian" is used in a variety of ways by various groups.

Meanings Change

Not only does the meaning of the word "Christian" differ from group to group, but it also changes through time. Hence, some of the apparent confusion over the use of the word "Christian" to describe the French can be traced to the evolution of the meanings associated with that term. For example, it has been well established that the first followers of Christ didn't call themselves *Christians*. They were first called *Christians* by outsiders as a derisive term (see 1 Peter 4):

> Originally the word probably meant something demeaning like "Messiah nut." But even this took place *fifteen years after* Pentecost. During this period and for probably quite a while later, they got along very nicely without calling themselves *Christians*. (Winter 1996:4)

By the nineteenth century the meaning of the label "Christian" had moved from something demeaning to include all who were born in a Christian country or of Christian parents (Webster 1828:37). In the twentieth century we find the word "Christian" indiscriminately used to identify the person professing belief in Jesus as the Christ, or the religion based on the teachings of Jesus, or simply a "decent, respectable person" living within Western civilization (Webster's 1970:253).

Most of the French men and women that we have had the joy of bringing to Jesus [2] can be used to illustrate the lack of evangelical meaning evoked in the French mind by the word "Christian." Before their personal encounter with the living Christ, the majority of these individuals would have used the following phrases to describe themselves: "I am French. I am Catholic. I believe in reincarnation. I am a Christian. I am an atheist. I am a scientist. I go to a healer when I am sick. I am a rationalist." As we will see in the next section of this study, when these people used the terms "Catholic" or "Christian" to identify themselves, it had little or nothing to do with what they believed or the nature of their worldview allegiance.

Is Western Europe "Post-Christian"?

We find the same kind of confusion over the meaning of the label "post-Christian" as we encounter with the word *Christian*. What exactly do missiologists mean when they say that a people group or country is "post-Christian"? Doesn't this term inherently assume that those it describes once were "Christian"? As far as Western Europe is concerned, some scholars question the legitimacy of such an assumption because they recognize that there has always existed a non-Christian Europe within the confines of historic Christendom (Luneau 1989; Wessels 1994). These scholars question whether large numbers of Europeans ever shifted their allegiance from their pagan roots when introduced to Christianity:

> The Church ... showed no disposition to trample on the paganism which it had supplanted. In many households the men remained pagan when their women-folk accepted the new faith; this continued as late as the time of Jerome, for some of his most notable disciples had pagan husbands. (Elliott-Binns 1957:399)

An examination of the situation in Italy, Spain, and France [3] after the collapse of the Roman Empire in the West reveals the persistent paganism which continued through the ages both outside and within the church:

> The old idolatry died slowly in the country areas of Italy. When Benedict came to Monte Cassino in 529 he found the peasants worshipping at a shrine of Apollo. The Lombards of the sixth century, although outwardly Christian, worshipped sacred trees and images of snakes. Pagan cults flourished in Sicily well into the seventh century. The Arianism of the Ostrogoths and Lombards in the Peninsula did not disappear until late in the seventh century.
>
> Spiritual conditions in Spain were very similar to those in Italy. Paganism and Arianism (in the case of the Visigoths) plagued Iberic Christianity as well as did the religious superficiality prevalent everywhere. Spain, apparently, never had had a solid evangelical basis for Christianity; rather she had had only the form of Christianity and a resultant worldliness that was destructive of spiritual effectiveness. ... The Christianity that soon was to face the onslaught of Islam was one of superstition, magic, and tradition; and although a part of the social fabric of the nation, it was devoid of spiritual power.
>
> ... The same was largely true of Gaul (France) in the early medieval centuries. (Edman 1949:177-178)

Furthermore, European observers note that non-Christian Europe has continued to exist, uninterrupted, to the present. One example of this phenomenon is the contemporary "New Right" grouped around Alain de Benoit which radically rejects the entire Christian tradition and calls for "a return to the 'authentic' pre-Christian roots of the West" (Luneau 1989:40). The permanence of this pagan tradition is emphasized by this neo-pagan writer, in his famous book *Comment peut-on être païen?* William Edgar, professor in Christian Apologetic at the Free Faculty of Reformed Theology, Aix-en-Provence, France, summarizes Benoit's position: "Paganism has never been far away from us, both in history and in the sub-conscious mind, as well as in ritual, in literature, and so forth" (Edgar 1983:308).

Not only does the term "post-Christian" tend to fool us into believing that past generations of Western peoples were truly evangelized, but it also can be understood to imply the total absence of a contemporary Christian presence. In other words, the term "post-Christian" does not sufficiently acknowledge the reality of a Christian remnant among the peoples it describes.

"Christendom" and "Post-Christendom"

The disconcerting conflict of meanings associated with the words *Christian* and *post-Christian* leads me to suggest that these terms should be eliminated from missiological vocabulary. They should be abandoned because the concepts they invoke reflect neither the biblical pattern of allegiance to Christ nor the spiritual state of the lands they describe. I propose that these terms be replaced with *Christendom* and *post-Christendom* to characterize the peoples of Western Europe. This seems to echo the position taken by Wilbert Shenk in an article written in 1994:

> For the sake of semantic and historical accuracy, we should distinguish between "Christian culture" and "Christendom." The latter is the correct synthesis forged by Emperor Constantine and his successors from 313 C.E. on, by which Christianity gained recognition as the religion of state, with the church functioning as the religious guardian. Christendom, or the *corpus christianum*, thereby became indistinguishable from society. Citizenship in society was synonymous with membership in the church, and baptism was a religiopolitical rite. It is quite another matter to judge the extent to which this religiocultural amalgam is truly *Christian* and can be deemed a faithful instrument of the reign of God in the world. (1994:8)

The words *Christendom* and *post-Christendom* refer to a historical, cultural, and spatial reality and its demise under the erosion of nearly two hundred years of secularization. When contemporary missiologists

and sociologists use the terms *Christian* and *post-Christian* to describe
Western peoples, I think that they are really referring to these historical
phenomena.

The Historical Reality of Christendom

It is commonly held that the conversion of Constantine marks
the beginning of Christendom in the sense of the identification of
the church with the whole of organized society (Dawson 1965:49-50;
Southern 1970:16). This is a feature of European history from the
fourth to the eighteenth century—from Constantine to Voltaire. [4]

Commenting on the influence of the Constantinian alliance of
church and state in Christendom, Southern writes:

> In an extensive sense the medieval church was a state. It had all
> the apparatus of the state: laws and law courts, taxes and tax-
> collectors, a great administrative machine, power of life and
> death over the citizens of Christendom and their enemies within
> and without. (1970:18)

Not only did the church wield statelike powers within Christendom,
but it also composed a compulsory society:

> From a social point of view a contractual relationship was estab-
> lished between the infant and the church from which there was no
> receding. For the vast majority of members of the church baptism
> was as involuntary as birth, and it carried with it obligations as
> binding and permanent as birth into a modern state, with the
> further provision that the obligations attached to baptism could
> in no circumstances be renounced. (Southern 1970:18)

If Southern's analysis is correct, then one might question the
extent to which individuals pledged voluntary allegiance to Christ
under Christendom. [5] Certainly some did. However, we have also
seen that pagan beliefs and allegiances also persisted beneath the
cultural surface of Christendom. The image is that of two streams
flowing simultaneously, one on the surface, in plain sight (Christianity);
and the other subterranean, hidden from immediate view (paganism). [6]
Thus, within the scope of Christendom, while many individuals
maintained their pagan allegiances and worldview, it was the church
which furnished the surface level of Western societies with their
spiritual values, their moral standards, and their conception of their
place in the universe:

> The church was much more than the source of coercive power. It
> was not just a government, however grandiose its operations. It

was the whole of human society subject to the will of God. It was the ark of salvation in a sea of destruction ... It was membership in the church that gave men a thoroughly intelligible purpose and place in God's universe. So the church was not only *a* state, it was *the* state; it was not only *a* society, it was *the* society—the human *societas perfecta*. Not only all political activity, but all learning and thought were functions of the church. Besides taking over the political order of the Roman Empire, the church appropriated the science of Greece and the literature of Rome, and it turned them into instruments of human well-being in this world. To all this it added the gift of salvation—the final and exclusive possession of its members. And so in all its fullness it was the society of rational and redeemed mankind. (Southern 1970:22)

Within the context of Christendom, to be *Christian* was to share a common tradition, common customs, festivals and sacrifices. This was associated with a territorial *Christianity* and a perception of human society which dictated that a single people must have a single custom. It is this understanding that enables the French to consider themselves "Christian atheists." When they say that they are Christian, it is like saying that they are French. It has nothing to do with faith and everything to do with identity as a people. By way of contrast, the label "atheist" identifies the nature of their faith (or lack thereof).

Thus, although Western civilization in Europe and America is the direct successor and heir of Christendom, we would be naive to believe that the inhabitants of these lands have embraced the person and precepts of Jesus of Nazareth and pledged Him their allegiance. The missiologist and historian of Christian mission, Wilbert Shenk, has affirmed that a study of literature, history, theology, and sociology reveals that the leitmotif running through the modern period is the bankruptcy of Christendom as an expression of Christian reality (1994:9). This view is shared by a former missionary to China who commented on the negative effect of this spiritual and moral bankruptcy on the emerging nations of the world which are seeing their own cultures being gradually transformed into Western culture. Comparing the spiritual condition of these peoples and that of countries once dominated by Christendom he wrote:

> The churches in the homelands of those early European missionaries are now sick and in their dotage. When Christians from the "younger" churches visit their "mother" churches, they are frequently shocked and puzzled. They often ask, "Why are we, the offspring of eighteenth- and nineteenth-century European mission, now so strong and growing while European Christianity

is weak, uncertain, and confused? Does a European fate await us if the main cause of European church frailty is the erosive effect of certain elements in Westernization?" (Beeby 1994:7)

The Need to Approach Post-Christendom France Missiologically

It is to be deeply regretted that the emphasis in Christian missions has shifted so very far away from the sense of duty and responsibility to effectively communicate the message of Christ to all peoples. While missional reflection and literature emphasizes "the uttermost parts of the earth," it frequently neglects "Jerusalem and Judea." Could it be that modern missiology has developed a blind spot here as a failure to appreciate the pervasive influence of centuries of Christendom on its own assessment of reality? [7]

Perhaps it is fear, not ignorance, that keeps us from acknowledging that post-Christendom lands are worthy candidates for missional reflection. Are we afraid that our task would seem too overwhelming if we made such an acknowledgment? In other words, if we can't consider *post-Christendom* peoples *Christian*, then we aren't faced with three impenetrable blocs of humanity (Muslims, Hindus, and Buddhists), but four! I suspect that our hesitancy to acknowledge our failure in post-Christendom lands could be that we fear that if our missional paradigms and ministry methods haven't really been successful at home, then ultimately they could fail overseas.

Bishop Lesslie Newbigin, recognizing that the Christian gospel has had rough going in post-Christendom lands in recent years because many Westerners seem to be inoculated against it, pleads for missiologists to apply their learning to this context:

> What we have is ... a pagan society whose public life is ruled by beliefs which are false. And because it is not a pre-Christian paganism, but a paganism born out of the rejection of Christianity, it is far tougher and more resistant to the gospel than the pre-Christian paganisms with which foreign missionaries have been in contact during the past 200 years. Here, without possibility of question, is the most challenging missionary frontier of our time. (1987:7)

Anyone who is serious about advancing the kingdom of God in post-Christendom lands must be willing to allow theology, intercultural studies, anthropology, history, and cross-cultural communications to question and inform his or her ministry. We must be willing to allow these disciplines to force us to take a fresh and critical look at the premises upon which we are operating and the methods to which we have become so accustomed. Above all, our missiology must deal responsibly with the realities of persistent paganism, historical Christendom, and the fact that God does indeed already have a people in these lands. The Old Testament prophet Elijah was ministering in a context not unlike that of contemporary Western Europe, and it is to his example that we now turn for instruction.

God's Whispering Witness

Elijah was living in a period of time which we might call "post-Yahwist." Before he ever came on the scene the people of Israel had begun worshipping two golden calves which Jeroboam had fashioned and set up, one in Bethel near the southern border of his kingdom, and the other at Dan, far up in the north (1 Kings 12:26-33). To further complicate matters, the pagan religion of the Canaanites, Baalism, which was not eliminated when the Israelites took possession of the land, had become the established religion of Israel. The real issues involved in this era are strikingly expressed by the names of the two principal figures: Jezebel, "Where is the Lord (god)?" (meaning Baal), and Elijah, "My God is Yahweh!" (Schedl 1972:47).

We read the very familiar account of Elijah's confrontation with the prophets of Baal on Mount Carmel in 1 Kings 18:16-40. At the close of a period of retirement and of preparation for his work Elijah meets Obadiah, one of Ahab's officers who had been sent out to seek for pasturage for the cattle, and bids him go and tell his master that Elijah was there. The king comes and meets Elijah, and reproaches him as the troubler of Israel. Elijah then presses for a divine confrontation. He proposes the verdict of Yahweh himself, on Carmel. It is then proposed that sacrifices should be publicly offered for the purpose of determining whether Baal or Yahweh is the true God. The king agrees to the proposal.

Herrmann gives the following rationale for the selection of Carmel as the site for this confrontation:

> The site of Carmel is particularly significant. It was part of the border territory disputed over by Phoenicians and Israelites. The king of Tyre had been able to extend his sphere of power this far south. Carmel may have had a sanctuary on it from earliest times, as was the case later. Even Tacitus mentions a sanctuary on Carmel, which was visited by Vespasian in AD 69. The place was ideal for

the worship of a mountain deity whose sanctuary could be reached easily, and at all times it must have attracted a wide circle of worshippers.

I Kings 18:30 also bears witness to the varied history of the cult place. Elijah reconstructed an altar to Yahweh which had been thrown down. So Carmel once had a regular cult of Yahweh, which seems most likely to have been instituted in the time of David and Solomon. But if that was the case, the divine inhabitant of this border area of Carmel must have changed under the influence of Canaanites and Phoenicians. Baal again predominated where once Yahweh had had an altar. (1981:210)

Rodgers observes that not only did this encounter take place in a place which the followers of Baal believed to be his dwelling place, but also the test was done with fire, which Baal worshipers believed was under his control:

Baal worshippers believed Baal was the god of fire and lightning. Now all the odds were in Baal's favor.

The Ugarit tablets contain some verses of Baal poetry which say that Baal carved his chateau from the rock with fire. *"The fire ate out the windows. The fire ate out the doors. The fire carved the corridors and the rooms."* The ancient Baal worshippers all believed that fire was used by Baal at his command. (1995:273)

On the one side stand the prophets of Baal, 450 in number, and on the other side Elijah, all alone. The prophets of Baal begin their ceremony in the morning. We can imagine that the rite begins with a long series of dances and prayers which last several hours. Gradually the dancing becomes more impassioned, and the prayers grow louder. By midday the priests are no longer in full possession of their senses; with swords and knives they wound their own bodies. This is not unlike the way in which various religious cults, sects and spiritist groups "condition themselves" today to receive messages from the spirit world and enter into a trance-like state.

The Hebrew expression used to describe their dancing means hobbling on both knees:

… such hobbling dances are described by Heliodorus in his description of Tyrian seafarers; they leap and skip, now darting upwards with sudden jumps, now squatting close to the floor and whirling around with the whole body, like possessed men. According to [1 Kings] 18:21, this hobbling (leaping) dance must have been a characteristic trait of the Baal religion: "To limp on both knees" is equivalent to "to serve Baal." (Schedl 1972:61-62)

I point this out to demonstrate the very deep involvement of the Israelites with this pagan religion. Theirs was no superficial mixture of paganism with true Yahwist faith. I believe that this ritual hobbling was a rite of spiritual empowering, whereby the demonic powers linked to Baalism were enabled and strengthened. The blood-letting of the pagan priests (apparently all Israelites) is another well-known form of sacrifice to occultic powers.

Until early evening Elijah waits patiently. Then, with the help of the assembled people, he rebuilds the ancient altar of Yahweh. Only then does he step forward and speak a short prayer. Immediately the "fire of Yahweh" falls from the sky (lightning?), with the result that the people fall on their faces, crying, "The LORD, he is the God!" Thus is accomplished the great work of Elijah's ministry. The prophets of Baal are then put to death by the order of Elijah. Not one of them escapes. Then immediately follows rain, according to the word of Elijah and in answer to his prayer (James 5:18).

When Jezebel hears of Yahweh's victory on Carmel, she vows to avenge herself on Elijah. Elijah flees for his life, taking the route into the wilderness to the south. Completely exhausted, Elijah rests under a broom tree where he waits to die. "I have had enough, Lord," he says, "Take my life; I am no better than my ancestors" (1 Kings 19:4). But then the angel of Yahweh calls to him: "Get up and eat" (19:5). He arises and sees, near his head, a cake baked on hot stones, and a jar of water. He eats and goes back to sleep. A second time an angel wakes him. After eating a second time, he walks, in the strength of the food, forty days and forty nights until he reaches Horeb, the mountain of God.

At Horeb Elijah apparently spends the night in the same cave in which Moses once looked upon the glory of Yahweh passing by (Exod. 33:22). What happens next is reminiscent of the experiences of Moses. All kinds of powerful, fear-provoking events are set loose: a mighty storm wind that breaks rocks into pieces, an earthquake, and fire. But Yahweh is not in any of these events. Then comes a still small voice (1 Kings 19:12).

Both immediately preceding and immediately following this encounter God asks Elijah the question: "What are you doing here, Elijah?" (vv. 9, 13). What *is* Elijah doing there? The Scriptures do not indicate that God instructed him to flee for his life. I think that Elijah is there because he is disappointed. He apparently thought that Israel would return to Yahweh after the powerful demonstration on Mount Carmel. Instead, he faced persecution. In the midst of that disappointment Elijah responds to God's question by twice affirming: "I have been very zealous for the LORD God Almighty. The Israelites have rejected your covenant, broken down your altars, and put your prophets to death with the sword. I am the only one left, and now they are trying to kill me too" (v. 10). At the end of this dialogue God gives Elijah a surprising revelation: "I reserve seven thousand in Israel—all whose knees have not bowed down to Baal and all whose mouths have not kissed him" (v. 18).

Based on Elijah's repeated statement that he alone was faithful to God (vv. 10, 14) and God's response in verse 18, I believe that his previous encounter with God in a "whisper," rather than in the mighty wind or raging fire, was intended to illustrate to Elijah the reality of what some have called "remnant theology." (The Apostle Paul would look back to this incident in his letter to the Romans and write that God did not reject his apostate people, but that even during his day "there is a remnant chosen by grace" [Rom. 11:4-5].)

In other words, God was communicating that He was at work in ways that were unseen to Elijah and through a people that remained hidden from Elijah's view. Elijah seems to have thought that God would work through dramatic "power encounters" to fulfill His purposes. Like so many of us today, Elijah had a preconceived idea of how God would operate to restore His apostate people. God seems to have been showing Elijah that He had a faithful remnant, barely a "whisper" in the midst of Israel, and that it was through that people that He was doing His work.

You have read the account in chapter 1 of how God showed to me that He has a remnant people within the French Roman Catholic Church. In the following pages we will see that others have made this same discovery. However, evangelical missionaries ministering in France differ in the weight they give to the faith and witness of this remnant people of God within the ancient Church in that land. There is no agreement on what might constitute our most appropriate response, as the cultural "outsiders" and "guests" in France, to the spiritual needs of the French. And many of us feel that it is necessary for us to establish "new churches" in France.

In the next chapter we will examine the realities of French culture. As we look at some of the attributes of contemporary French society that make our task of announcing the gospel message extremely difficult, it is important to keep in mind that the situation is not hopeless. While we might be tempted to lament with Elijah that we are God's only voice in France, we must not forget that God has reserved for Himself a "remnant" people in that country.

Notes

1. (p. 12) A walk through the office of the Dean of the School of World Mission at Fuller Theological Seminary demonstrates the dearth of missional reflection and research directed toward post-Christendom peoples. The walls of this office are lined with bound copies of the dissertations done by students of this school, grouped according to the area of the world which they investigate from a missional perspective. A simple count of these dissertations reveals the following: 269 dissertations deal with missiological issues in an Asian context; 132 dissertations are concerned with Africa; 75 with Latin America; 40 with North America; 35 with Oceania; and only 22 with Europe.

2. (p. 13) It is noteworthy that on three occasions Andrew brings others to Christ: Peter (John 1:41), the lad with the loaves (John 6:8-9), and certain Greeks (John 12:22). These incidents may be regarded as a key to his character and provide us a glimpse into the purpose of all missional activity.

3. (p. 14) The pages of Gregory of Tour's *History of the Franks* presents a vivid impression of the sad spiritual state in Gallic Christendom:

    The enervating consequences of religious polemics against Arianism in the church, violence and witchcraft in the court, abysmal ignorance among the masses, religious quacks announcing themselves as Messiahs, brutality and coarseness, church support by corrupt kings, paganism in rural areas, superstition in the Church with its worship of relics, usually spurious, and blind credence in miracles, equally; such factors made a mockery of Christianity. (Edman 1949:178)

4. (p. 16) The breakdown of Western Christendom is a process extending over several centuries involving a variety of factors. Dawson, for example, feels that it began in the seventeenth century with the loss of Christian unity through religious divisions, followed in the eighteenth and nineteenth centuries by the abdication by Christians of their responsibilities with regard to certain fields of social activity (1965:19). He explains that this process varied from society to society within Christendom, but that in all Western lands the outcome of the last two hundred years' development has led to similar results:

    This process was a complex one. On the continent of Europe, especially in France, it was a violent and catastrophic change, which involved political revolutions and religious persecutions. In England on the other hand, it was extremely gradual and piecemeal and even today some of the typical institutions of the old Christian order, like the State establishment of the national Church and the solemn religious consecration of the monarch, still survive. The case of America, or rather the United States, differs from each of these types. ... However, the traditional Christian civilization has now become a part of history and can only be understood by a considerable effort of study and imagination. (1965:37)

5. (p. 16) It is not only Protestant evangelicals who define legitimate Christianity in terms of voluntary allegiance to Christ. Father Bob Bedard, Director of the Catholic Renewal Center in Ottawa, explains that true conversion involves a deliberate choice of allegiance to Christ:

> It involves making Jesus the Lord of my life and entering thereby into a personal relationship with him. I begin to know him in a deeper and more intimate way.
>
> Evangelization, therefore, is the process whereby a person hears the gospel, embraces it fully, makes Jesus Lord of his life and gets involved in a lively, intimate and ongoing relationship with him.
>
> ... Paul VI would agree with this kind of definition. In the encyclical mentioned, he spoke of the "radical conversion" to the Lord that the gospel requires (*Evangelii Nuntiandi* 10). He spoke of the necessity of the "... profound change of mind and heart" that full evangelization involves.
>
> The present Holy Father says the same thing. Evangelization calls, he teaches, for a deliberate "acceptance of the Good News" (Puebla, Mexico, 1980). When he adds, "God's action requires our response" (ibid.) he just about says it all. (Bedard 1996:3)

6. (p. 16) In a fascinating article on Europe's neo-paganism Marc Spindler points out that its background is the crisis of Christendom as well as a crisis of all cultural patterns and political models that have inspired life of Europeans in the last twenty years:

> Neo-paganism has its prophets: Nietzsche, who died in 1900 but whose "gospel" is still widely distributed; Hermann Hesse, another German writer quoted by W. A. Visser 't Hooft. In Great Britain we have, for instance, Julian Huxley, Aldous Huxley, and especially D. H. Lawrence. In France, one of the first was André Gide (*Les nourritures terrestres*, 1897); then Victor Segalen (*Les immémoriaux*, 1908), Antonin Artaud (*Le théâtre et son double*, 1938), Georges Bataille (*Acéphale*, 1937), and many other successful writers, such as Céline, Montherlant, and Jean Cau. These writers, however, offer a pagan spirituality, no pagan program. The new development is the emergence of a definite movement with a pagan program, with paganism as the central motive. This movement has been called the New Right, but this is a political classification that I consider largely irrelevant. Neo-paganism is a religious choice, and only a religious choice of another kind is a proper reaction to it. Anyway I want to stress the importance of this movement in Europe today. W. A. Visser 't Hooft even asserts that "European culture has become a debate between three forces: Christianity, scientific rationalism and neo-pagan vitalism." (Spindler 1987:8)

7. (p. 18) Loren Mead has emphasized the dramatic transformation of missional thinking that took place when the church became officialized under Christendom (1991:10-12). Prior to the conversion of Constantine the relationship between the church and the surrounding "hostile" world was characterized by its witnessing activity. Under Christendom the world that immediately surrounded the church was legally identified with the church. In other words, there was no clear boundary between the world and the church. During the pre-Christendom, Apostolic understanding, the missionary frontier was the world immediately surrounding the believer. However, under the influence of Christendom the frontier into mission lay at the border of political and geographical conquest.

It is evident that we continue to be influenced by the Christendom understanding of mission as something that takes place in far-off pagan lands. However, Mead contends that Western lands have entered into a post-Christendom reality:

> The environment of Christendom has changed: we can no longer assume that everybody is a Christian; people no longer assume that the community is a unity of the religious world, living out the values derived from the Gospel; we are returning to one of the features of the Apostolic Age, and we now assume that the front door of the church is a door into mission territory, not just a door to the outside. (1991:25)

Chapter 3

The French: Familiar But Puzzling

One of the most disconcerting qualities of the French is their apparent ability to live contradictory realities at the same time. In the last chapter we saw that many of the French, influenced by historical Christendom and its demise, claim to be Catholic and atheist at the same time. To the North American such an affirmation seems both illogical and unlivable. This is but one of many apparent contradictions of the French.

I have lost count of the times when North American tourists have mentioned to me the cold reception that they have received from the French. Over and over again I am told that the French are rude and unwelcoming. To many foreigners it is not surprising that the patron saint of Paris is St. Genevieve, a nun who fasted and prayed in the sixth century to keep Paris safe from foreigners. She fits an image that France cannot shake off. All studies show that outsiders look on the French as the coldest and least welcoming people of Europe (Taylor 1990:15).

Yet there are few countries in the world that have welcomed and embraced so many foreigners, from the Italian Renaissance genius Leonardo da Vinci to the Spanish painter Pablo Picasso to the Irish writer James Joyce to the African American singer Josephine Baker.

Some of the most celebrated French of the twentieth century, such as Nobel prize-winning physicist Marie Curie, actor-singer Yves Montand and novelist Roman Gary, were born outside France.

Sally Taylor opens her book about the French with the words: "The French have peculiarities that can frustrate anyone no matter what their cultural expectations" (1990:7). However, Americans are especially puzzled and frustrated by the French. Their apparent con-

26

tradictions seem even more enigmatic because the French, we think, ought not to be so puzzling. To an American, the French are not really exotic like the Australian Aborigines or the Maya or even the Japanese. French culture seems familiar. French champagne and perfume and cheese and ballads and movies conjure up old and warm images. Yet, although Americans sometimes feel they have France within their reach, they rarely grasp it. No other people so similar to us seems so different than us.

The Reality of Culture

It is a "mood," a "spirit," a "unique way of viewing the world" that sets the French apart from others. This is what anthropologists call "culture." And as George Peters, Professor of World Missions at Dallas Theological Seminary, acknowledged:

> Culture is a stern reality. It is as extensive as man and as comprehensive as his ways, thoughts, sentiments, and relationships. It is the all-encompassing non-biological atmosphere of his being as well as the institutions that make his life tolerable and mold him into the being he actually is. (1981:193)

I don't think that the French are any more suspicious or unwelcoming of foreigners than any other people in the world. For the North American who encounters French culture, however, there is a clash because the French, especially in Paris, are not an open, gregarious people like Americans or Latinos. They are taught to be inward and undemonstrative. Their societal norms dictate that they be slow to commit themselves and not show their feelings openly. This kind of behavior is considered polite and correct in France.

I am reminded of an incident that occurred a number of years ago. My wife and I returned for a short visit to the United States after spending six or seven uninterrupted years in France. On our way from the airport in Los Angeles to the place where we would be staying, we decided to stop for a bite to eat. After we took our places around the table in the restaurant, a young waitress brought us all a glass of water and inquired about our day. She was cheerful and smiling as she said in a rather loud voice, something like: "Hello! How are you all doing today? Isn't it a beautiful day?"

To which I caught myself thinking: "You hypocrite! You don't really care how we are doing!" That was a typically French way of responding to what they consider to be North American naiveté.

You see, what American cultural norms consider to be correct ways of demonstrating friendliness, the French interpret in a completely different manner.

However, most of the French are not defensive, intolerant and insensitive. Most are not rude (even though this is how our North American culture interprets their way of relating to others). It is true that most French do not open up quickly to people they do not know, whether foreign or French. But once contact is made and renewed, they are as kind and loyal as any other people. They show their friendship and emotion.

I use this example of miscommunication to illustrate the importance of culture. We have already seen that French culture has been shaped by the realities of historic Christendom and persistent paganism. What follows is a brief treatment of some of the most dominant aspects of French culture and how they affect missionary endeavors. It is not designed to be exhaustive, but it is a place to begin. We followers of Christ, perhaps more than any other group, should face the need to understand culture. This is an imperative. It is a challenge that faces every generation of God's people, for, as Joseph Aldrich has stated:

> Many of the practices of Western Christianity are cultural. As such, they may be useful and effective. Unfortunately, however, many cultural patterns are counter-productive and actually work against the evangelistic enterprise—not to mention the truth of the Gospel … note this important, crucial principle: The greatest barriers to successful evangelism are not theological, they are cultural. Many of our culturally determined patterns of life keep people from Jesus Christ! (1981:40)

The Principle of Incarnation

As missionaries, to ignore the dynamics of French culture is to ignore reality and biblical responsibility. The example and teaching of our Lord Jesus Christ compel us to incarnate the gospel message in such a way as to penetrate effectively the French society with His "Good News." Jesus became flesh in a specific time-space setting. There were cultural implications. For Jesus the incarnation meant not only a new expression of His divine nature, but it also meant a *Jewish* human expression of His nature. It meant not only a new way of life and a new lifestyle, but it meant a *Jewish* way of life and a *Jewish* lifestyle in a *Jewish* culture and with *Jewish* customs. It also meant subordination in a *Jewish* family setting. The Apostle Paul sums it up succinctly: "For I tell you that Christ has become a servant of the Jews on behalf of God's truth" (Rom. 15:8). Imagine that: Christ a *servant* or *slave* of the Jews!

The Apostle Paul apparently took a similar approach in his own ministry:

> For though I am free from all *men*, I have made myself a slave to all, that I might win the more. And to the Jews I became as a Jew, that I might win Jews; to those who are under the Law, as under the Law, though not being myself under the Law, that I might win those who are under the Law; to those who are without law, as without law, though not being without the law of God but under the law of Christ, that I might win those who are without law. To the weak I became weak, that I might win the weak; I have become all things to all men, that I may by all means save some. And I do all things for the sake of the gospel, that I may become a fellow partaker of it. (1 Cor. 9:19-23 NASB)

The examples of Jesus and of Paul show us that in respect to culture, the messenger must change, rather than the hearer of the message. The Scriptures indicate that the message of Christ must be spelled out in a cultural time-space setting. Christ must become incarnate in many cultural forms. Paul made Christ incarnate in Gentile-like form in order to reach Gentiles. Aldrich makes the following insightful analysis of Paul's relationship to the various cultures he encountered:

> Let's examine Paul's evangelistic strategy, particularly as it relates to the various cultures he ministered in and through. In I Corinthians 9:22 he writes, "I have become all things to all men so that by all means I might save some." Note first of all how important "becoming" is in the task of "saving some." To win the Jew he "became" a Jew. To win those under the law, he "became" like one under the law. To win some, he became all things to all men (vv. 20-23). In fact, he became a slave to "everyone," to win as many as possible (v. 19).
>
> Note carefully that evangelistic effectiveness is directly related to the ability to "become," the ability to understand and relate to social and cultural differences. To the Jew he became a Jew. To reach them he honored their noble institutions; he regulated his social life. He refused to blast his way through custom and conscience. I am certain he limited his liberty when it was appropriate. He did not appeal to the Gentile out of the Old Testament world view of the Jew. He didn't practice the Mosaic law among them or make it the basis of his preaching. It was totally foreign to their

culture and life style. He tempered his brilliance and power when
dealing with the weak. He never willingly insulted their beliefs
and prejudices.

The issue at stake is not what I need to know, as much as what
I need to "become." The critical question is not "What information
do I need to master?" as much as, "What identity do I need to
assume?" The radical difference we have talked about must be
"biblical" if evangelism is to be effective. To be radically different is
not to be self-righteous, legalistic, and withdrawn. To be radically
different is to be like Christ. This is our identity and the key to a
redemptive identification.

Paul's efforts to adapt his life and method to the target audience
underscores the fact that every effective decision for Christ must be
made within the framework of "their" culture if it is to be genuine.
Paul's strategy focused on stressing points of likeness rather than
difference ... whatever evangelistic strategy we use, it must fit the
environment into which it is directed. (1981:69-70)

The examples of our Lord Jesus Christ and of the Apostle Paul
demonstrate that we missionaries cannot be satisfied with anything
less than the most perfect kind of adjustment to the cultures in which
we find ourselves. Complete identification, or at least as perfect an
identification as possible, is necessary for the gospel to be incarnated
into French society. We cannot be satisfied with being merely a "good
friend," for our calling demands us to be "all things to all men," and
to "empty ourselves" of the ways most familiar and natural to ourselves and thus become servants of our adopted people (Phil. 2:6-7).
Not "our dear friend" but "one of us, our servant" is what our French
neighbors must say of us.

Only a thorough understanding of the nuances of French culture
will unveil for us the true meaning of "becoming all things" to the
French. We must learn how to remove the barriers created by our own
cultural background that keep us from truly entering their world.

Again I point to Jesus Christ as a model of one who witnessed
across the boundaries of culture and societal groupings without
establishing unnecessary barriers. In John chapter 4, verses 9 and 27,
we learn that the disciples were shocked to discover Jesus bridging
the cultural gap between Himself and the Samaritans. Nothing in
them related to the hated Samaritans, who held wrong doctrines,
polluted their race with Gentile blood and were enemies of the Jews.
All the disciples saw that day was the hardness of the Samaritans and
their distance from the truth. In much the same way many evangelical
Protestants view Catholics today. Jesus, however, in essence declared,

"The Samaritans are a harvest field that is ripe" (John 4:35). The problem was not the Samaritans, but the hearts of Jesus' followers.

Had Jesus shared the opinions of His disciples He would not have ministered to the Samaritans. Any arrogance or pride of nation, race, culture, status, or even religion would have kept Jesus aloof from the Samaritans.

Notice also that when the Samaritan woman inquired where one should worship, Jesus lifted worship above specific forms and places, stating that the time was coming when they would neither worship in the mountain of Samaria nor in Jerusalem, but the important thing was to worship God in spirit and in truth (John 4:22-23). Jesus presented Himself to the Samaritans as the Messiah-Savior, but significantly He left the physical forms of worship a blank page.

One could wonder whether the testimony of the woman would have received the same results among the townspeople (John 4:40) had her message been: "He told me everything I ever did, *and he commands us to worship God as the Jews of Jerusalem do.*" Would the townspeople have been able to receive Jesus, or would their own religious prejudices have kept them from discovering that "... this man is the Savior of the world" (John 4:42)?

How were the Samaritans to worship their new-found Messiah the following week? Isn't Jesus really saying, "The outward forms you use in worship of me may change and pass, as I say they are not critical; the glory of my incarnation is that I delight to be incarnate in varied and different worship forms, so worship in the form in which you feel freest, as long as you worship the Father in spirit and truth"?

French Patterns of Culture which Preclude Belief in the Gospel

Culture can be defined as the total life-way and mentality of a people. [1] We missionaries do not deal with French culture in the abstract but with individuals who live in a specific society and who share a common way of life. One of the most common pitfalls that could overcome us in our attempt to analyze missional activity in France is the tendency to lose sight of the uniqueness of cultures. Every culture has, so to speak, a personality or individuality of its own. We must avoid the tendency to give identical interpretations to behavioral patterns whenever and wherever superficial similarities are found to exist between North American and French culture.

In order to come to grips with the dynamics of ministry in post-Christendom France we must begin by answering certain questions. Questions like: What is particular about French culture? How do the French differ in their thinking, behavior and attitudes compared with other peoples? What are some of the factors that affect all of the French, young and old alike, consciously as well as unconsciously? In what ways are the French unlike all the other peoples on earth?

Secularization

We have already noted that the establishment of Christendom did not do away with the paganism that had previously existed in France. Sociologists and missiologists point to a number of causes for the secularization of Western culture. Since the late Middle Ages, developments in European philosophy and science have depicted an increasingly autonomous sphere of human knowledge and activity purged of supernatural presuppositions. The Enlightenment exalted human reason and removed God further from European life. Nineteenth-century changes accelerated the trends. Revolutions against political authority called into question divine authority. New political configurations sparked anticlerical political factions which, in France, were extremely violent. Industrialization and urbanization moved the masses away from nature and away from rural religious patterns. Liberalism in thought led to skepticism. Higher criticism undermined the authority of the Scriptures. These secularizing forces affected most of Western society, but led to different types of secularization.

In France, generations of religious and ideological conflict led to what some have labeled "utter secularity," devoted to the destruction and replacement of Christianity. The vehemence of French secularity explains why in post-Christendom France, which has been marked by centuries of Christendom, many people today are not open and receptive to the teachings of Christ.

Yet change is in the air in France. In his book entitled *Francoscopie*, Gérard Mermet writes:

> Having arrived at the sunset of a Century unlike any other, France has also arrived at the end of a period of her history, and even at the end of a type of civilization. Real mutations have taken place during the last thirty or forty years that are, without doubt, more weighty than all those of the past ... The previous social system and mentalities have recently been destabilized and have produced what seems at first glance to be the collapse of values. What we have witnessed is, in reality, the inversion of the foundations upon which rested collective and individual life. (1995:12)

If you are interested in reading a description of some of the "new foundations" that are replacing the former values of French society, see Appendix A.

Sophistication

We must not allow the cultural sophistication, education and advanced technology of the French to hide their enormous spiritual needs. Bruce Babcock writes: "Although theirs is a rich and industrious nation, France has become one of the most demanding of mission fields. Underneath all the glitter and sophistication lies a tremendous spiritual problem to which only the Gospel can respond" (1988:1).

Missiologist P. J. Johnstone observes about France:

> One of the world's most cultured and sophisticated nations is reaping the fruit of 200 years of secularization. Barriers to the gospel are many—intellectualism, rationalism, widespread involvement in the occult, individualism and a nodding acquaintance with institutional Catholicism ... France is not only needy, but also hardened to the gospel. (1986:177)

Lack of a Strong Biblical Tradition

For years American missionaries working in France have been attempting to identify those traits of French culture which determine the way the French respond to their message. In the next chapter we will examine some of the reasons why the French have been resistant to our many evangelistic attempts and why ministry methods which have proved to be so successful in the United States usually fail in France. However, at this juncture it is important to acknowledge that one of the most clearly felt differences between French and American culture is the absence of a strong biblical tradition within French culture:

> The missionaries were surprised by the French unfamiliarity with the Bible. They often needed to convince Frenchmen that the Bible had not been written by the Protestants. Missionary files abound with references to Frenchmen who had never heard of the Bible, and letters from mayors, teachers, and even nuns who had received their first Bible by responding to a missionary brochure. (Koop 1986:143)

Indifference

Another attribute of the French that has bothered missionaries is their apparent indifference to the gospel message. According to Babcock,

"Today in France, a profound ignorance of the Bible accompanies profound indifference to the claims of Christ" (1988:5). Robert Evans, who ministered in France for nearly forty years, wrote:

> While there were cases of overt and covert opposition to the missionary activity in France, the missionaries were far more disturbed by the indifference with which most Frenchmen met their efforts. Even the few who showed interest normally declined to make a definite commitment. The common expression *je ne voudrais pas m'engager* ("I don't want to commit myself") terminated many evangelistic discussions. (1963:130-131)

For many of the French, religion seems to be disconnected from the realities of contemporary life. They think that it is irrelevant. On the other hand it must be noted that the French are profoundly spiritual. Jacques Ellul, former professor of history and sociology of institutions at the University of Bordeaux, France, in a lecture to English-speaking missionaries (September 9, 1970, Bièvres, France), entitled "What You Need to Know About France in Order to Serve God More Effectively There," stated:

> The French—even the free thinkers, even the skeptics—are religious. But not necessarily Christian. There are other religions: it is a mistake to think that once we have spoken of Buddhism, Islam, etc., we have exhausted the list. Obviously this is not the case!
>
> Not only are there new religions, but there is also a return to the old ones. In the French countryside everybody lives according to magic and sorcery. I am well acquainted with this phenomenon. I can point out to you precisely where witchcraft is practiced in centers of peasant sorcery near Bordeaux. One farmer who knew very well that my wife and I were Christians suddenly announced to me as we sat in front of a winter fire, "There you are, that is God. There is no other God!" And he was absolutely serious! His religion was the worship of fire. Later I learned that worship of fire among farmers in that area was on the increase.
>
> But this phenomenon is not confined to rural areas. Magicians, fortune-tellers, astrologers, palm readers, and horoscopes in every newspaper are part of city life. ...
>
> Fundamentally, we are not speaking as Christians to dechristianized rationalists, but rather to a population belonging to another religion or to other religions. So our task is no longer to convince a man who believes nothing, but rather to confront believers in other gods: that is, to face precisely the same situation as in the Old Testament or at the time of the Apostles. (1986:21, 23)

The French Tendency to Contest and Split into Factions

Many missionaries who have stressed the basic incompatibility between French culture and evangelical Christianity have mentioned certain traits of French character, such as French morality (or lack of it). Another French characteristic which is often mentioned by Americans and French alike is the French emphasis on individualism. Americans are accustomed to teamwork and an ethic which fosters individual sacrifice for group success. The French, on the other hand, are more often than not unwilling to relinquish their individual interests for the sake of the group.

John Ardagh, in his study of contemporary French culture, points out that "... for every initiative that succeeds [in France], there are several others that fail. And the cause, as often as not, is the French tendency to contest and split into factions. As one Frenchman put it: 'Give the French more autonomy and they abuse it by splitting into factions'" (1982:641). This tendency is a result of the preeminence of secular humanism in French culture:

> In proposing an ethos for his generation, Camus exalted what he called "the rebel": ... self-appointed saviors, men who see themselves as substitutes for God. ... Camus belongs to an old moralistic tradition that stretches back through several centuries of France's intellectual life, and that embodies much of the Enlightenment spirit that has so powerfully marked modern France over the past two hundred years. ... So long as the various currents of rationalistic humanism continue to run strong in France, and so long as from time to time they bring us a voice as compelling as that of Albert Camus, that heritage will continue to shape the nation's outlook and destiny. (Wright 1974:462-463)

Ardagh closes his book by observing that the French continue to be "argumentative, hedonistic, highly competitive, full of energy, also egotistical and in some ways still conservative. They are still as aware as ever of their own French individuality" (1974:654).

French Culture Has Been Marked by Roman Catholicism

Perhaps when we speak of "Catholic France" we should use the term "subsociety." A society may include a number of subgroups, each within its own traditions. This is particularly true of the more complex societies. These subsocieties not only share the common culture and history of the larger society, but they also possess their own historical development and have their own ways and values, their own customs and mentality. For example, in the United States we have one society and one way of life which, however, embraces a relatively large number of subsocieties and subgroups. The Jews, Protestants, Mormons, and Catholics constitute distinct subgroups within the American society. They possess distinct traditions, have their own *esprit de corps*, but at the same time they share a common American tradition and group spirit.

The concept of "subsociety" has an important bearing on practical apologetics and communication. French Protestants and French Catholics form two different subsocietal groups of French culture. When attempting to explain our evangelical views to a French Catholic we must not only cross the cultural boundaries that separate us as peoples, but we must also cross the boundaries that separate us as members of two different religious subsocieties. Hence, just as the American missionary, wishing to understand the Frenchman, must realize that he or she does not speak the same cultural language, likewise the evangelical Protestant attempting to communicate with the Catholic must acknowledge that he or she does not speak the same subsocietal language. Each subsociety has its own way of life and underlying assumptions, values and goals, and unless the communication is geared accordingly it will fail to inform, convince and persuade.

The unbelieving Catholic community of France is the subsociety of French culture that we are attempting to reach for Christ. This group is the dominant subsociety of French culture, comprising a little less than 70 percent of the entire French population.

Although the average Frenchman does not practice his Catholic faith, it is an integral part of his identity. Recent studies have demonstrated that although most of the French neglect the Catholic Church almost entirely except at the crucial moments of christening, marriage and burial, a high percentage of French people still pay lip-service to Christianity through social convention (see Appendix B). More importantly, THE MAJORITY OF THESE PEOPLE STILL CONSIDER THE CATHOLIC CHURCH TO BE *THE* CHRISTIAN CHURCH! For these individuals, Jesus and his followers were Catholics.

The missionary who will come to grips with French culture must discover how to evangelize in a context where everybody says he or she is Catholic. We cannot sidestep the issues of culture if we are calling men and women to conversion, as John R. Stott so succinctly points out:

Conversion is not the automatic renunciation of all our inherited culture. True, conversion involves repentance, and repentance is renunciation. Yet this does not require the convert to step right out of his former culture into a Christian sub-culture which is totally distinctive. Sometimes we seem to expect him to withdraw from the real world altogether.

In both the West and East it is vital for us to learn to distinguish between those things in culture which are inherently evil and must be renounced for Christ's sake and those things which are good or indifferent and may therefore be retained, even transformed and enriched. (1975:122)

When we demand that a Frenchman renounce his Catholic sub-culture (subsequent to conversion), we are seen as undermining the fabric of traditional French society, and are thus regarded as dangerous fanatics and provoke fierce, irrational hostility. There have been examples of this kind of accusation against the followers of Jesus of Nazareth since the earliest days of the Church, as when the Jews accused Stephen of teaching "that this Jesus of Nazareth will ... change the customs which Moses delivered to us" and when some merchants of Philippi accused Paul and Silas of "disturbing our city" because "they advocate customs which it is not lawful for us to accept or practice" (Acts 6:14; 16:20-21). In both cases, although one context was Jewish and the other Roman, the issue concerned "customs," either the abandonment of old customs or the introduction of new ones. [2] Culture consists of customs, and people feel threatened when customs are disturbed.

Of course, in one sense Jesus Christ is always a disturber of the peace, because he challenges all inherited custom, convention and tradition, and insists that the whole of life must come under His scrutiny and judgment. Yet it is not a necessary part of our mission as His followers to destroy French culture (or even Catholic subculture) for no better reason than that it was part of a French person's pre-conversion experience. Because mankind is God's creation, some of human culture is rich in beauty and goodness. Because mankind is sinful and fallen, all of human culture is tainted with sin. So cultures, and human societal systems and subsystems, must always be tested and judged by Scripture, yet no human culture is to be fully rejected.

If this is true, then our freedom to operate as missionaries in post-Christendom France is restricted by three forces: the principles of Scripture, the realities of French culture, and the presence of a dominant Catholic subsociety in which God has a remnant people. It is only as our approach adapts to these three considerations that we can minister in Jesus' name without compromising the Word of God, without becoming offensive as Americans, and without becoming divisive as Protestant evangelicals.

Addressing missionary endeavors within a Muslim background, Bishop Kenneth Cragg sums up well the relationship between conversion and culture when he writes that conversion "is not 'migration,' it is the personal discovery of the meaning of the universal Christ within the old framework of race, language and tradition" (1956:336). We will look at this again; however, at this point there is one last aspect to be developed before we leave our discussion of culture. This is an important consideration which merits our attention.

We Must Avoid the Temptation to Impose Our Evangelical Protestant Subculture on the French

The World Evangelical Fellowship recognized this danger and responded to it by declaring: "We must acknowledge that often we have also set our evangelical traditions above Scripture. In many instances our lip-service to biblical authority contradicts the predominant place we give to our denominational and historic baggage" (1986:25). In the same way that we must avoid imposing American lifestyle on the French, neither can we permit ourselves to force Protestant evangelical identity or practice on them.

When our Protestant evangelical practices become too important to us as missionaries, the message which is often received by the French (even if it is not explicitly stated by the missionary) is: *to be saved you must accept Jesus Christ as your personal Savior and Lord, and become one of us, an evangelical Protestant.* Such a message is clearly not biblical, as the Apostle Paul points out so well in his writing to the Gentile believers dwelling in Galatia. We know that he was writing to Gentiles, for he says, "Formerly, when you did not know God, you were slaves to those who by nature are not gods" (Gal. 4:8). This evidently refers to idolatry, and we know that the Jews of Paul's day were not idolaters. The Apostle in this letter essentially says that for anyone to impose Jewish customs and laws on Gentile followers of Christ is tantamount to making those customs and laws necessary for salvation! In which case they would be on a par with Jesus Christ. Paul rightly rejects this legalistic notion. His teaching indicates that religious practices become legalistic when:

1. They are equated with Christ as a means of salvation.
2. They are imposed upon another culture. (For example, when French or American evangelical subcultural practices are imposed upon members of the French Catholic subsociety.) This is tantamount to making those practices equal with Christ, for the hearer in the other culture is obliged to practice the imposed culture as well as receive Christ, thereby communicating that the alien religious practices are as important as Christ.

The fifteenth chapter of Acts is a mighty declaration that under no circumstances should Jewish religious practice be imposed upon Gentile followers of Christ. [3] Rather, Christ would sanctify and become incarnate within Gentile culture, removing its evil aspects (Acts 15:19-20). The question in Acts 15 is whether Gentile believers would have to adhere to the Jewish religio-cultural practices, and in respect to this, the words of the Apostle James are simple and beautiful: "It is my judgment therefore that we should not make it difficult for the Gentiles who are turning to God" (Acts 15:19). It is my opinion that the imposition of evangelical Protestant identity and practices on those who hear our message in France makes it "difficult" for those who would turn to God!

It is obvious that James was saying that the witnesses of the gospel in the New Testament era should not burden the Gentile converts with Jewish religio-cultural forms. But what about the Jewish followers of Jesus? We know that Judaism was replaced by the faith community (composed of the followers of Christ) as the channel of God's grace and salvation to humankind. Therefore, would not the Jewish religious practices have to be discarded as legalistic? Wrong! The Apostles Peter and John, with Christ at the center of their lives, went regularly up to the central Jewish Temple, evidently to pray. Moreover, it would have been pointless for the Jewish followers of Jesus to meet and deliberate about whether or not Gentile believers had to keep Jewish religious forms of worship (as recorded in Acts 15) if the Jewish believers were not keeping them. The evidence is strong that the Jewish followers of Christ continued to observe the Jewish religious practices with Christ right at the center, giving fullness and meaning to their religious experience, and causing their Jewish worship forms to be fresh and alive with His presence.

Today we see a return to this type of witness of Christ through Jewish religious practices used by Messianic Jews, and we see many more Jews embracing the person and precepts of Jesus of Nazareth than we ever did when we insisted that they abandon their Judaism and become "Christian." In like manner some missionaries who used to feel strongly that all Roman Catholic religious forms and practices had to be discarded when a French person responded to the call of Christ are beginning to change their position. These present-day witnesses to the gospel message realize that the Frenchman's religion so entwines his culture that to strip him of his religious heritage means stripping him of his cultural identity as well. However, the tragic scene described by Grace Brethren missionary Kent Good is all too common: "When you become a Christian in France, you have to abandon part of what it means to be French. Being Catholic is as much a part of being French as being born in the country. So you have to give up a lot" (1986).

It seems to me that this position not only violates biblical principles governing cross-cultural communication of the gospel, but it also ignores the tremendous power society holds over the individual member of a given culture. I believe that failure in this area explains the dismal results of missionary endeavors in France in the past decades. It is to the history of recent missionary endeavors in France that we now turn.

Notes

1. (p. 31) Luzbetak states:

> To define culture is no easy matter. In fact there seem to be as many definitions as there are anthropologists. One of the earliest definitions was that of E. B. Taylor: 'Culture or civilization is that complex whole which includes knowledge, belief, art, morals, law, customs, and many other capabilities and habits acquired by man as a member of society' (1874:1). Lowie defined culture in much the same manner: Culture is 'the sum total of what an individual acquires from his society —those beliefs, customs, artistic norms, food-habits, and crafts which come to him not by his own creative activity but as a legacy from the past, conveyed by formal or informal education' (1937:3). Some of the definitions formulated are as simple as 'total social heredity' and 'tradition,' while others are far more complicated. Kluckhohn proposed the simplified formula 'culture is the total life way of a people, the social legacy the individual acquires from his group' (1949a:17). Gillin suggested that culture consists of patterned and functionally interrelated customs common to specifiable individual human beings composing specifiable social groups or categories' (1948:181). Keesing sums up culture as 'the totality of man's learned, accumulated experience which is socially transmitted, or, more briefly, the behavior acquired through social learning' (1958:18). (Luzbetak 1970:4)

2. (p. 37) The missionary must be careful not to communicate the wrong message by his mode of behavior or lack of cultural participation. The question that we must continually ask is: What does this activity mean to the people? As Erickson has pointed out:

> Cultural events and objects have no intrinsic worth, but rather have the value and significance attributed to them by the common mind of the society. It is not so much the object or the action, in many cases, as it is the meaning of the object or the action. ... The Christian in society must so contextualize that the right meanings are delivered through the cultural forms and ideology. (1978:80)

3. (p. 39) Norman Erickson, Professor of New Testament at Trinity Evangelical Divinity School, makes the following pertinent observations concerning Acts 15:1-29:

> The prominent example of contextualization in the Christian church centers around the council at Jerusalem. Conflict had arisen because of the many Gentiles who gladly received the gospel of Jesus Christ. Certain persons at Antioch insisted that in order to be saved the brothers had first to be circumcised according to the custom of Moses (Acts 15:1). On the other hand certain believing Pharisees insisted that *after* believing it was necessary for the Gentile believers to be circumcised and to keep the law of Moses (Acts 15:5). There are two issues at hand in this discussion. The first regards the method of salvation for Gentiles: Is circumcision compulsory? The second question follows on a negative answer to the first: What are the conditions for table fellowship between Christian Jews and Christian Gentiles?
>
> The incident at Antioch, as reported in Galatians 2:11-14, clarifies the second question. Peter, most likely in response to his vision and the Spirit baptism of Cornelius (Acts 10), was willing to have fellowship at table with Gentiles. But when he heard of the offense this gave to Jewish Christians in Jerusalem, he separated himself in deference, not to the Gentile Christians, but to the Jewish Christians who were complaining. Paul, from the perspective of the believing Gentiles, insisted that Peter (and Barnabas) were play-acting by doing for approval what they knew to be nonessential.
>
> The result of the conference at Jerusalem is a declaration, not that Gentiles must be circumcised or keep the Mosaic law to be authentic Christians, but rather of the minimal courtesies which would allow fellowship between believing Jews and believing Gentiles. ...
>
> There are three observations to be made here: (1) the Gentiles were not compelled to observe circumcision or other "customs" of Moses; (2) the Jewish Christians were not compelled to *stop* circumcising, nor to stop observing the Mosaic customs; (3) the context for the declaration by letter is one of deference to the Gentile Christians and was established for the purpose of table fellowship between Gentile Christians and Jewish Christians. (1978:74)

Chapter 4

Learning from Our History

In order to understand my insistence that we think missionally about ministry in post-Christendom France, we must consider briefly the history of evangelical Protestant missionary activities in that land. Our understandings should be guided first of all by "God-breathed" history—the revealed Word of God itself. However, great portions of the Bible contain historical accounts of the way God has dealt with His people. The Apostle Paul wrote to the New Testament believers at Corinth and said, "These things happened to them as examples and were written down as warnings to us, on whom the fulfillment of the ages has come" (1 Cor. 10:11). Today, both the Old Testament and New Testament can assist us to refocus our thinking, as can the history of the Church through the ages.

However, of particular interest to us is the history of evangelical Protestant missionary activity in France. The best study to date on the subject of North American mission work in France is Allen Koop's book, *American Evangelical Missionaries in France, 1945-1975*, upon which this chapter is based.

American Evangelical Protestant Missionary Activity in France Before 1945

American evangelical Protestant missionary activity in France before 1945 was very limited. Until the Second World War, most American believers assumed that European churches were capable of carrying out the task of evangelism in their respective countries. The 1910 Edinburgh conference on missions, which set the tone for mission work in the early twentieth century, did not consider Europe a mission field. Even during the war, when Americans were concerned about Europe, calls for missionary activity in Europe were rare (Kellar 1942:228).

A Brief Summary of American Evangelical Protestant Missionary Activity in France Since 1945

Koop observes that the end of World War II revealed the weakness of the French church. Not only had church buildings been destroyed, clergy and laity killed and congregations dispersed during the conflict, but the war and occupation had opened the eyes of some to the pervasive de-Christianization of French society (1986:21). H. Godin's book, *La France: Pays de Mission?*, published during the war, revealed the extent to which the masses of France had deserted the Roman Catholic Church (Ward 1949). Cardinal Suhard's pastoral letter, circulated at the end of the war, dealt soberly with the challenge of a declining church. The World Council of Churches published conclusions of convincing case studies which confirmed the notion of total de-Christianization in various geographical areas and social classes. Koop observes that subsequent studies marshalled more documentation to contend that urban France was "basically pagan":

> American church historians Kenneth S. Latourette and Martin Marty later agreed. French religious sociologists moved into rural France, and while noting significant regional variation, forced the conclusion that "a complete picture of religious vitality in France would show that at least four-fifths of the population have no contact with the Christian church, and live in total ignorance of the Gospel." Concerned Catholic voices were joined by conservative Protestant leaders like Bordeaux social scientist Jacques Ellul. The French, he claimed, had abandoned Christianity for political and materialistic substitutes: "Christian concerns became simply irrelevant, and Christian words (piety, salvation, grace, redemption) awaken no echo in the modern French mind." (1986:21)

When the first American evangelical Protestant missionaries arrived in France at the close of the war, they agreed with the conclusions drawn by the Protestant and Catholic leaders. The France that they discovered was indeed de-Christianized. What they failed to come to grips with was the fact that, even in de-Christianized (post-Christendom) France, the Catholic Church influenced society and dominated religious life.

The evangelical Protestant missionaries simply regarded all Catholics as "lost souls who needed to be converted in order to be saved." In fact, as far as many of these missionaries were concerned, being Catholic was far worse than being simply unchurched, for, as one of these evangelical Protestants put it in a recent letter: "Being Catholic was to live a lie, a lie which would only be exposed at death, when the unsuspecting person ended up in hell for believing that he could work himself to heaven by good deeds." Not only did these missionaries make little or no attempt to accommodate or even understand the various factions of belief and practice within French Catholicism, but they also felt obligated to share the "real truth" with Catholics they met. The overwhelming majority of these missionaries were convinced that they "had Jesus." And the Catholics didn't. It was as simple as that.

This attitude crippled the efforts of these missionaries. They failed to measure the impact of nearly two thousand years of Christendom. As we saw in the last chapter, even today nearly 70 percent of the French continue to identify themselves as Catholics. At the end of World War Two as many as 85 percent of the French people were identified with the Catholic Church (at least through baptism), and for most of these individuals to be a follower of Jesus Christ or religious meant Catholicism.

Missionary Relationships with French Protestants

Koop also points out that the American evangelical Protestant missionaries experienced difficulties in their identification with French Protestants. These difficulties grew out of the fact that Protestant strength in France was very small (approximately 2 percent of the population) and concentrated in a few regions: Alsace-Lorraine, the Cévennes and Bas Languedoc area, the lower Rhône valley, the Charente and Paris. Even more important to the American evangelicals was the theology of the French Protestants:

> Except for a small conservative minority, French Protestant leaders traditionally maintained liberal theological principles which were anathema to evangelicals. ... The missionaries kept their distance from these people. Even though the Catholics considered regions of France as mission fields, most French Protestants resented the evangelical implication that France was a mission field, and they were amazed to find missionaries among them. (Koop 1986:24)

Missionary Relationships with French Evangelicals

Fortunately, within French Protestantism were the French evangelicals, and with these the Americans felt doctrinal compatibility. However, if Protestant numbers in France were small, evangelical numbers were tiny. Jacques Blocher, a leader in French evangelical circles, referred to them as a minority within a minority. And, unfortunately, this small section of French society was never known for its unity: "Divided unevenly into no fewer than thirty-seven groups, the French evangelical community was too fragmented to speak with one voice" (Koop 1986:25).

Moreover, while the missionaries shared the theological persuasions of this small group of French believers, and spoke the same religious language, the relationship between the two groups was often difficult. The American missionaries often complained that they found the French insular in outlook, bereft of vision, and prone to bickering. The French occasionally proved unreceptive to criticism or even aid from the recent arrivals from the New World (Koop 1986:26).

Evangelistic Endeavors

What was the activity of these missionaries? Koop points out in his study that they "merely attempted to repeat programs which had been successful in the United States" (1986:27). Then he uses nearly 150 pages cataloging, group by group, the history of each particular evangelistic endeavor.

He points out that the missionary work met with something less than universal acclaim. In fact, the French often criticized the evangelical Protestants in their evangelistic enterprise as being frothy, superficial, sensational and unstable. Koop states that "although some of the converts became sincere evangelicals (a few became pastors), most drifted away" (1986:29).

Involvement in the French Catholic world has allowed me to see that many Catholic leaders view North American evangelical Protestant missionaries and their activities as naive, insensitive, or even arrogant. I can illustrate this from my own experience. I am ashamed to have to admit that when I arrived in France I felt that "God arrived with me." The idea that He could already be at work in that country and that I needed to "find out what He was already doing and then join Him" was foreign to my thinking. How arrogant I was! How naive and insensitive! Even after I discovered that God has a remnant people in the Catholic Church, I still felt that I had everything to offer and nothing to learn from them. How sad!

In the next chapter of this study we will see how the activity-orientedness of North American evangelical Protestant missionaries is actually an element that makes them seem "foreign" or "cultish" to the French. Whenever we don't know how to proceed we fall back on the activities of the past. This seems to be a human characteristic. For a number of years I observed French Catholic catechists fall back on the known activity of an organized "pilgrimage" and "weekend retreat" when they couldn't figure out how to advance in their ministry to junior high school kids. In the same way, American evangelical Protestant missionaries have been wedded to traditional ministry methods like children's classes and street preaching, even though these achieve only limited success. For example, they have attempted to do some tent evangelism in spite of the fact that tent evangelism, born on the American frontier, is not attractive to French people.

Another alternative open to the American evangelical Protestant missionaries was to become involved in the evangelism of children. Missionaries who felt uncomfortable in a new culture often found it more satisfying and less demanding to work with children rather than adults. One of the couples on our own ministry team became enamored of this approach to ministry in France. Koop remarks that the basic concept of the evangelization of children has a history of meeting resistance in France:

> Infant baptism and first communion were usually thought to fulfill the church's role to children. ... The attempt to persuade a little child to renounce the family religion (or the family's opposition to religion) could provoke great opposition. It made the missionaries appear to be intent on dissolving the French family unit. (1986:33)

The impact of evangelical radio programs in France has also been severely limited because commercial stations usually air the programs only between midnight and six in the morning. Gospel posters struggle with a similar narrow impact. Distribution of literature yields little in France. Koop found that normally there was only one response per thousand leaflets distributed (1986:53).

You can imagine how this lack of receptivity to traditional evangelical Protestant activities was discouraging to the missionaries. Koop makes the following pertinent observation:

> Convinced at first that the job of evangelizing France could be completely accomplished in a decade, the success-oriented Amer-

icans were forced to come to terms with under-achievement. ...
Discouraged by their slow progress in French culture, the American missionaries generally concluded that the work and time
necessary to produce one convert in France would yield ten or
even twenty in the United States. (1986:44)

Church Planting, More or Less

The majority of the American evangelical Protestant missionaries
who have come to France since World War II have come to do what
they call "church planting." This means that the newly arrived American "pastor" goes door-knocking until he finds a handful of converts;
then they proceed to meet and call it "church."

The church growth movement in North American Evangelicalism
is largely responsible for inspiring this approach. This movement
has offered a "how-to-do-it" approach to ministry that fosters both
confidence and frustration. The confidence comes from the assurance
that one has a clear ministry strategy. However, the frustration soon
follows when missionaries in France compare the results of their own
church planting and church growth efforts with missions in other
parts of the world. Koop points out that the church growth movement
finds its roots in a historical context that is foreign to the French:

> The Americans were so anxious to get a church started, and so
> proud of their achievement once a tiny church was organized,
> that they failed to realize that their small success made greater
> success less likely. The evangelical missionaries came from a
> culture which accepted and even took pride in small independent
> churches. Many midwestern towns supported a different church
> on each street corner. The French saw things differently. For them,
> there was only one church; or perhaps two in regions where
> Protestants were visible. Everything else was a sect. They lumped
> together all little religious groups, no matter how divergent their
> beliefs: Adventists, Jehovah's Witnesses, Friends of Man, Men-
> nonites, Brethren, Baptists, Salvation Army, Pentecostals, Christian
> Scientists, etc. *In American history small dissenting sects had grown
> into major denominations. While not all sects became large churches,
> most large churches had started as sects. In France, the relationship between
> sect and church was antithetical, not evolutionary.* Sects remained
> outside the center of traditional French religious culture, and so
> did the sectarian missionary churches. Nonetheless ... the search
> for strategy took most American missions in France to the policy
> of establishing small indigenous churches. (1986:86-87, *emphasis mine*)

It is easy to imagine not only the frustration of the American evangelical Protestant missionary force, but also their disenchantment as their quest to discover a solution to their problems proved futile. As the number of missionaries in France continued to grow, so did their attrition rate as a number of missionaries abandoned their plans to serve in France.

Reliable information on the number of departures from France and on the exact reasons for departure is virtually impossible to obtain. Sometimes the decision to leave was made for family reasons such as the education of children. Sometimes there was a call of a more productive ministry in the United States to which the missionaries returned. But more important than the actual figure was the widespread notion that France was a mission field which claimed many casualties. And whatever the primary reason given for a missionary departure, underlying many decisions to leave France was the frustration caused by the discouragingly slow progress, as Koop so aptly demonstrates:

> Highly motivated and optimistic in their decision to go to France, the missionaries often found it difficult to cope with the failure to fulfill their aspirations. Amid reports of the encouraging success of missionary work around the world stood the stark reality of the often stagnant work in France. Continually rebuffed in door-to-door distribution, laboring in tent campaigns to which few French people came, struggling with groups which failed to grow or even coalesce, the missionaries felt either personal spiritual inadequacy or cultural unadaptability or both. (1986:95)

It has been common for American evangelical Protestant missionaries in France to change the nature of their work and even their mission affiliation. Teachers would become church planters, church planters would become teachers, street evangelists would go into radio work. The change sometimes reflected the missionaries' clearer perception of how they might be more effective in French society. But more often it was discouragement, not perception, which prompted an abrupt change in activity (Koop 1986:88). The history of American evangelical Protestant missionary endeavors in France is clearly more often characterized by struggle than by glowing success.

The following excerpt from a letter, written by an international lawyer with years of experience in France, to a missionary couple preparing for ministry is informative:

> I have seen many outreaches to France fail over the years, so I know what you are going into. I have seen marriages fall apart,

children fall into cracks, and finances disintegrate. This is what I mean by failure. Ministry can happen, but if the missionaries or mission team dissolves from within, they come home in defeat. ...

Few of us here in the U.S. realize that France has been rated by *Operation World* as the second-hardest country to evangelize. For your entire service in France you will have to learn to battle the presumption that yours is a not too taxing assignment. No one will bestow you with the automatic support and sympathy given to missionaries serving starving bands of refugees, or working with orphans, or smuggling Bibles and holding secret prayer meetings in communist or Muslim countries. Your satisfaction will come in knowing, that without recognition or accolade, you are reaching out to a people whom the Enemy has convinced that God is a farce, that Christianity is a mythology steeped in desperation, emanating from cultural emptiness. ...

So there are three problems which have plagued the American evangelical Protestant missionaries in France. First, conversions, rare as they were, often failed to lead to church membership. Second, much of the church growth that did occur was transfer growth. And, finally, the American missionaries to France found that their new churches were often based upon foreigners.

Why Has the Progress of Missionary Activity in France Been So Slow?

Why has American evangelical Protestant missionary activity proved so futile and evangelistic progress been so slow? What lessons can we learn from the experiences of the mission groups who have been ministering in France since the end of World War II?

The Position We Take Towards Roman Catholicism Is Determining

First, we can realize that mission work in France is unlike mission work anywhere else in the world. French culture is unique, and will require a unique approach, a different strategy, other methods than we have used elsewhere. If we are unable to adapt our methods and strategies to the realities of French society we are in for a very rough time.

Secondly, it is evident that in France, our position towards Roman Catholicism will determine how we are perceived by the majority of the French. This fact has been recognized by missionaries ministering in France since the sixties:

> By the 1960's most missions realized that they had to achieve status in France by identifying themselves with some Christian group in French society. The missionaries never considered identifying themselves with the largest Christian group in France, Roman Catholicism. On the contrary, their intense doctrinal opposition to Catholicism compelled them to stress their distance from Rome. (Koop 1986:171)

Babcock writes that even today the French assume all non-Catholic groups to be cults: "Therefore, most Frenchmen see no difference between evangelical Christians and Jehovah's Witnesses, for example. As we share Scriptures with our friends we continually strive to relieve their suspicions of our activities and purposes in France" (1988:5).

Our Struggle Is with Catholic Subculture

Dr. J. Herbert Kane, the late Professor Emeritus of the School of World Mission and Evangelism at Trinity Evangelical Divinity School, expressed the necessity to reexamine our evangelistic and church planting strategies in Catholic Europe with the following words:

> So we have little choice. Either we minister to thousands of receptive, needy, hungry people within the parishes and help build up the Body of Christ in a very needy part of the world (and thus undermine the myth of the cult) or we do our own thing and end up with a handful of converts hardly large enough to organize a viable local church.
>
> There will, of course, be those who object to the fact that the new converts are remaining in the state church or the Roman Catholic Church. This does, indeed, pose a problem: but what shall we do?
>
> The question is: Is it better to leave the Roman Catholics and state church members in Europe without the truth of the gospel and allow them to perish in their sins or to teach them the Word of God and build them up in the Christian life, knowing that they may very well remain within the state church or Roman fold? (1986:2)

Most American evangelical Protestant missionaries in France realize that although our numbers are growing, our persistent efforts have yielded small results. We all want to make an impact on France; however, many of us now feel that our only impact will be upon the lives of some individual Frenchmen. And, while we believe in the immeasurable worth of a single "lost sheep," it is still difficult to take comfort in this kind of achievement. We must continue to evaluate our efforts in the hope of finding the reasons for our many failures.

Some missionaries take a long view. They compare our missionary experience in France with that of China, where the first generation of missionary work produced little, but was followed by years of broad expansion and significant achievement. While I admit that my experience in France is limited, France is not China, and I feel the comparison to be inappropriate for at least two reasons. Firstly, upon their arrival in China, the first Protestant evangelical missionaries discovered a people who had never heard of Jesus Christ. While we have identified a wide stream of paganism running through the history of the French, even under Christendom, it is also true that there has been an evangelical witness to Christ in France continuously through the centuries. This was not the case for China when the missionaries first arrived there in the nineteenth century. Secondly, in the decomposition of historic Christendom we are now confronted with the formidable task of presenting the person and teachings of Jesus to people who reject the church (which represents Christ) and yet consider themselves to be "Catholic Christians."

Some American evangelical Protestant missionaries in France feel that the problems can be overcome by energy, hard work, efficient organization, and effective leadership. I am convinced that the problems that we are facing in our ministries in France are deep and complex. I do not feel that simply trying harder will do; the gulf that separates us from those we are trying to win to Christ is too great. Thomas Julien, Director of European Missions for Grace Brethren Foreign Missions, in his address to the Foreign Workers Conference held at Aix-les-Bains in 1969 put it this way:

> I think that our difficulty is deeper than most of us are willing to admit. It is the tremendous gulf that separates us from the people we are trying to reach.
>
> The gulf is cultural. Evangelical Christianity in France, even among our French brethren, is essentially Anglo-Saxon in its expression. The gulf is intellectual. Most of us find ourselves intellectually inferior to the people we are trying to reach, and to compensate, we reach a class of people who have little influence on others. It is philosophical. We live in a world of absolutes and they do not. And we have found a way to speak to them meaningfully only if they accept our absolutes. It is linguistic. We speak French poorly, and often fail to realize that the Frenchman hears our words in a different frame of reference than ours. The gulf is social. We have few real social contacts with the French. We are tense in unfamiliar situations. The gulf is religious. We often communicate the external trappings of our particular brand of Christianity. ...

Perhaps the success we see in our work is not because we are necessarily bridging the gulf, but because some of the French people are willing to leap over to our side in order to have Christ. (1969)

In the following chapter I will propose some ideas on how we can begin bridging some of these gulfs that separate us from the French. It is evident that we cannot allow ourselves to continue eschewing relationships or identification with the major Christian denominations in France. While I refuse to suggest new ministry methods or models, I do think that by adopting a new missional paradigm and examining the visibility of our approaches we can significantly alter the way we are perceived by the French. If we do not make the appropriate and necessary adjustments in our ministries we will continue to work against the grain of European history in the twentieth century. As Koop puts it: "While the French converted empty churches into garages, the American missionaries converted garages into churches" (1986:178).

Chapter 5

Friend, Foe, Ally ... or Servant?

How can we evangelize the French? Or how can we launch a new movement within the Catholic subsociety of French culture that is characterized by New Testament life and vitality? To what extent are we to allow the spiritual, cultural and historical realities that we have dealt with thus far in this book to shape our approach to the ministry in France? These questions continue to guide our thinking as we complete almost two decades of ministry to the French.

When we began our missionary service in France in 1979, we had only a vague idea of how God might lead us to minister there. At that time we fixed as our objective the "development of Christian communities in France characterized by common purpose, mutual involvement in each others' lives, and group worship." Although we were not altogether certain as to the structure that these Christian communities would adopt, we felt that they would probably be largely like what we had experienced in the United States.

Shortly after our arrival in France in the fall of 1979, the man who founded the ministry of the Navigators in France, Dean Truog, gave us the following counsel: "Be very careful in defining your relationship toward the Catholic Church ... this seems to be a major factor determining the effectiveness of an evangelistic ministry in France." When we first received that counsel we did not realize its importance. It was not until after we had ministered for several years in France that we began to weigh its significance.

During the ensuing couple of years as God led us into increasing contact with Catholics and into a deeper understanding of the dynamics of French culture, we found ourselves obliged to re-examine our basic presuppositions concerning the "church planting" model that we had adopted.

This chapter is modified from my article: "A Model for Analysis of Incarnational Ministry in Post-Christendom Lands," Missiology XXV, 3 (July 1997): 279-291.

In 1982 the overseas director of our mission wrote me a letter asking: "What are you guys doing in France? Are you going to start a Missionary Church or not?" In response to his inquiry I wrote:

> We find ourselves confronted with the dilemma facing every Protestant missionary working in France. Are we going to insist on identity with the Missionary Church for these converts, and thus become ineffective in evangelism and divisive of the Body of Christ? Or are we institutionally humble enough to put God's purposes above our own? Will we continue to allow these French men and women to come to Christ through the small Bible discussion groups? Or will we begin erecting unnecessary barriers by insisting that they identify with the Missionary Church?

The problem confronting evangelical Protestant missionaries in France will not be resolved by finding new and better methods for the propagation of Christ's message. Its answer does not lie in the implementation of more dynamic, seeker-friendly, North American evangelical forms of worship. I believe that the realities of ministry in post-Christendom France call us to reexamine the foundational premises of our missional paradigm and the activity orientation of our approach.

Let's Take a New Look at Missions

Seventeen years of experience as an evangelist, disciple maker, and church planter in France has convinced me that ministry in post-Christendom lands presents the missionary community with challenges and opportunities that call into question the most widely accepted of our missional paradigms and many of our methodologies. This is particularly true for the evangelical community whose witness for Christ in Western Europe is often ineffective because our governing missional paradigm and our ministry methods, working in conjunction, tend to project a separatist image and isolate us from those we wish to reach for Christ.

My goal is to discover an effective missionary approach to post-Christendom peoples. As I attempt to combine elements from my own missionary experience and reflection, I sense that a tool can be developed to enable us to gauge the extent to which a given missionary endeavor is seen as "culturally appropriate" by the receptor culture. This level of "cultural appropriateness" can be correlated with the degree of resistance to our message by the people we are attempting to reach for Christ.

Recognizing that every missionary enterprise is delimited by the governing assumptions of its underlying paradigm and made visible to the receptor society by its methods, I suggest that we can measure the relative strength of these forces and identify four different types of missional ministry in post-Christendom lands resulting from their combination.

I will begin by reflecting on the two major missional paradigms that are available to us as we minister in post-Christendom France. The "Church-centered paradigm" and the "Kingdom of God paradigm" are the poles of a continuum along which all current ministries in France can be placed. I will demonstrate that these paradigms do indeed define the nature and goals of our ministries and determine their effectiveness.

Ministry methods also decide the efficacy of our outreach. Ministry methods presently used by missionaries in France can be located on a continuum stretching between the two poles of "Formal" and "Relational."

Paradigms in Conflict

On my arrival in France I felt that my ministry goal of leading French men and women to personal faith in Christ and banding them together to give birth to self-supporting, self-governing and self-propagating evangelical churches was the correct missional response to the French situation (Hodges 1971:128). I assumed that the church either did not exist in France, or that if it did exist, it was so weakened and compromised by its history that it should be replaced. The fact that Europeans recognized the need for missionaries in their lands strengthened my resolve. And, although the strategies developed by the church growth movement had met with very limited success in France, my commitment to the objective of planting independent evangelical churches was unshaken (Koop 1986:109).

At the same time I became aware of growing ferment within Francophone Catholic circles, partly in response to the appeal of John Paul II for the "re-evangelization" of Europe. As my understanding of contemporary French society grew I began to realize that a good number of Catholic leaders were deeply concerned by the nominal religious adherence of most of the French (Wessels 1994). I also learned that many of these men and women recognize that the community of faith needs to be "reborn" in many different localities in France and within most of the segments of French society (Suenens 1992; Carrier 1993).

Monsignor Gilson, the Bishop of Le Mans, typifies these individuals. He once explained to me that, whereas in the past French people grew up in the Christian faith and discovered Christ because they were born within Christendom, today this is not the case. He observed that French men and women were all too rarely brought to faith in Christ by the sacraments and liturgy of the Church. His conviction, shared by a good number of French bishops, is that people must first be brought to faith in Christ before they can discover the Church. He is deeply concerned by the areas in his diocese where the Church has ceased to exist as a community of faith.

The discrepancies between the assumptions of my missional paradigm and the reality I discovered in France bothered me. I wondered: Is it really necessary for me to establish a "new church" in France? How seriously should I take the faith and witness of the ancient church in this land? What would be my most appropriate response, as the cultural outsider and "guest" in France, to the spiritual needs of the French? My inner turmoil was calmed only as my missional paradigm moved away from the church-centric model to an understanding of ministry in the light of the kingdom of God. [1]

The kingdom of God paradigm, based on the simple statement of John 20:21, is different in many ways from the church-centered concept under which I had been operating. Whereas the church-centric model encourages individual groups of believers to assert and develop themselves, [2] the kingdom of God model stresses the cross. It is a radical perspective that encourages living out the truth that "we do not preach ourselves, but Jesus Christ as Lord, and ourselves as your servants for Jesus' sake" (2 Cor. 4:5).

Rather than being "church-centric," [3] the kingdom of God paradigm is centered in the person of Jesus, sent from the Father, empowered by the Spirit. It is in Jesus' crucifixion and resurrection that the missionary enterprise must take its start, find its methods and define its goal (John 20:21-22). Mission, seen from the perspective of the kingdom of God, flows out from the cross of Christ, is characterized by the cross (Phil. 2:5-8; 1 Cor. 9:19ff.; 2 Cor. 4:5), and results in the application of the cross (Luke 9:23; Rom. 12:1-2, 14:7-11; Gal. 2:20). [4]

The kingdom of God paradigm, like the church-centered paradigm, requires that the sending church dispatch missionaries who are ready for self-emptying of their westernness in order to plant churches that are a "thing of the soil." However, unlike the church-centric paradigm, the kingdom of God paradigm proposes that when missionaries are going to a post-Christendom land, such as France, their self-emptying must also include a stripping, or putting aside, of their ecclesiastical rights and privileges. The indigenous church-centric paradigm, as it is understood and applied today by many missionaries in France, serves to reinforce the ecclesiastical rights, theological distinctives and self-awareness of each group of believers, whereas the kingdom of God calls us to willingly put the emphasis elsewhere.

The Power of a Paradigm

What we understand determines what we choose to do. And what we choose to do makes all the difference in the world in the missionary enterprise. The following comparison contrasts the practical ramifications of these two paradigms:

Church-Centered Paradigm	Kingdom of God Paradigm
Message	**Message**
Conversion is often understood as becoming a follower of Jesus and joining *our church*.	This paradigm recognizes that members of God's kingdom are to be found within the state churches; conversion involves becoming a follower of Jesus and joining a *community or network of believers*.
Focuses on the group's doctrinal distinctives, the observance of what the group considers to constitute the essential forms of worship, and its particular system of pastoral government.	Focuses on worldview allegiance to Jesus Christ as the central issue and allows for a certain amount of diversity within the boundaries of "supra-cultural" truth.
The convert changes his or her identity to "become one of us."	The goal is to change the convert's understanding of his/her previous identity (so that in France, for example, he or she would experience a "ratification" of his or her baptism).

Missions

Has the same goals for ministry in post-Christendom lands as it has for ministry in pre-Christian countries, i.e., the "Three-Self formula."

The missionary agency is self-promoting in that it seeks to establish an indigenous church "after its kind" in foreign soil.

Reinforces a "fragmented" view of the kingdom of God based on the idea of ecclesiastical independence.

Establishes its own "indigenized" sacraments and liturgy.

Adopts an analysis of the spiritual needs of the country based on the contemporary situation.

Missions

Allows the goals to be determined by the particular needs of the church which already exists in post-Christendom lands.

The missionary agency sees itself as the "servant" of the existing Body of Christ.

Reinforces the universal scope of the kingdom of God based on the ideas of interrelatedness and interdependence.

Teaches converts to appreciate the established (indigenized?) sacraments and liturgy of the existing church.

Adopts a broad view of the situation with appreciation for what God has been doing in the country through the ages.

Missionary Spirituality

The missionary tends to view himself/herself as "one who has arrived" at a better, more thorough understanding of the truth than the one held by the leaders of the state church. The emphasis is on the product.

The missionary sees himself/herself as a church-planter who is beginning the true church in virgin soil.

Missionary Spirituality

The missionary takes serious account of the believers who are already present in post-Christendom countries. The missionary is a "pilgrim" who has things to both offer to and learn from the existing church. The emphasis is on the process.

The missionary sees himself/herself as one who proclaims the kingdom in word and deed, inviting men and women to submit themselves to the Lordship of Christ.

Formal Versus Relational Methods

It is often our choice of methods that determines how we are perceived by the members of the society we are trying to reach for Christ. The testimony of Tom Julien, formerly Director of European Missions for Grace Brethren Foreign Missions and missionary to France for twenty-eight years, illustrates this reality: "When we first came here," says Mr. Julien, "we spent three weeks with a team of thirty people. We put tracts everywhere; we visited every house in the area; we had a dozen or so meetings in rented homes; we had meetings in the streets, and as a result of all this, we had nobody." Not only did his group not find open hearts, but they closed many doors of opportunity: "We probably created more barriers that we are still trying to break down. We created an image of a cult rather than allowing the glory of the gospel to shine through the life of a person" (1986:5).

Koop agrees that our formal, highly visible, activity-oriented ministries in France actually communicate the wrong messages to the French people, thereby making our mission exceedingly more difficult (1986:44-46, 86-87). The following table summarizes the major differences between relationship-oriented and formal, activity-oriented ministries:

Formal [5]	Relational
Evangelism	**Evangelism**
Something one "does." It becomes centered around special events like the Sunday Celebration or evangelistic meetings.	A lifestyle that influences everyday encounters with others. All of life's circumstances and situations become vehicles for the communication of our Christian hope.
Something that is done only by specially gifted members of the church. Anyone can witness, but it takes uniquely gifted individuals to introduce people to Jesus Christ. Hence the need to organize events where one brings friends to whom witness may or may not have already been given.	Something every member of the Christian community is involved in because that is how followers of Jesus live. It is always going on "behind the scenes" as laypeople are sharing their faith and their lives with their acquaintances and friends.

Discipling

Takes place in a "Sunday School class" environment with little in-depth one-on-one mentoring involved. The group is promoted and continues to exist even though the members may change.

Group Identity

The identity of the group is extremely important. The desire is to be "known" in the community as a "truly Christian" group (often in opposition to other groups). The highly visible activities are, more often than not, organized around a "Worship Celebration" (regardless of the day or time of the week on which this group gathers).

The group is centralized around an established meeting place such as a community center, transformed garage, or church building. This "place" of worship and fellowship is tied to the identity of the group and hosts the most important of its activities.

Growth

Numerical growth is relatively easy to measure since it occurs as the Lord "adds to the group those who would be saved," and they, in turn, join in the activities of the group.

Discipling

Takes place in one-on-one mentoring relationships and in small groups. The group exists for the strengthening of the individual members and has no identity or life of itself.

Group Identity

The individual Bible study groups do not have a name or identity of their own. They might exist on either the inside or the outside of the existing parish structures. There is low visibility of the group, with high visibility of the lives and witness of the individual members of the group.

The group is decentralized in the sense that it grows out of the "street" or the "marketplace." The homes of the believers are the most important places where ministry takes place because that is where the most intimate of life's experiences are lived.

Growth

Numerical growth is difficult to measure because it occurs as the converts reproduce their lives in the lives of others (2 Tim. 2:2). There is no centralized "gathering" of these converts to reinforce their ties to the missionary agency.

A Model for Analysis of Incarnational Ministry in Post-Christendom Lands

Now that we have considered the two dichotomous pairs of missional paradigms and methodologies, it is time to place them together to form our analytical tool. (See Figure 1.)

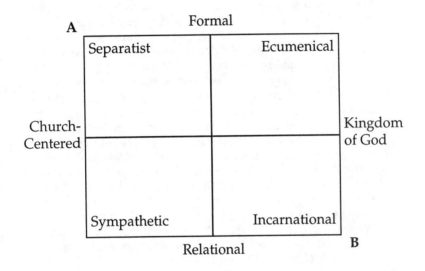

Figure 1

Analytical Model of Incarnational Ministry

As with any analytical tool, the missional paradigm/missionary methods model has inherent strengths and weaknesses. The application of this model is not intended to reduce the contextualization of the gospel in post-Christendom lands to a simple four-variant matrix, but rather to enable missionaries ministering in such places to compare and contrast their own approaches to the other possibilities. The missional paradigm/missionary methods model provides conceptual glasses through which we may discover new perspectives on the incarnation of the gospel in countries marked by Christendom.

Separatist: Church-Centered/Formal

Separatist missionaries understand their mission in terms of individual conversions, with the implied aim of gathering believers into self-supporting, self-governing, and self-propagating churches on the basis of a closely defined statement of faith. [6] One reason why this view of their mission makes perfect sense to these missionaries is their reluctance to acknowledge the legitimacy of the ancient church in de-Christianized lands (Koop 1986:22, 171). The following words, written by Jacques Blocher in 1966, express the commonly-held view of the evangelical community in France:

> We strongly emphasize the fact that churches may become apostate even if they retain the name of a Christian Church. In some of them the teaching of the Word of God has been adulterated to such an extent, that a born-again Christian can scarcely be expected to grow in grace and prosper and serve, *if he does not break away and unite with a church in which God's truth is effectively proclaimed.*
>
> The church of which the writer was pastor for many years in Paris has a majority of its membership composed of former Roman Catholics. For many of them *it was very difficult to leave their old church, but they could not do otherwise. I am certain that there are some real Christians within the Roman Church, but their difficult struggle for survival is a proof that their position is to be regarded as exceptional.* Our statement remains valid! The Roman Catholic system hinders the spiritual growth of a born-again Christian. And it is to be feared that Rome is not the only Church of which this is true ... We know that from the apostolic time until today proper missionary evangelism will inevitably involve change of religious adherence. (1966:119-120; *emphasis mine*)

While their position makes sense to these missionaries, it often results in suspicion and real harm. For over three years I met once a week for a time of prayer with a French parish priest. One morning when I arrived at our appointed place of prayer I found my friend visibly troubled. After I pressed him to tell me what was bothering him, he reached into his drawer and pulled out a tract which he slid across the desk to me. The tract had been placed in his mailbox (and in the mailboxes of all of his parishioners) by an evangelical group whose address was rubber-stamped on the back. The tract urged all its readers to "save themselves from hell and the Anti-Christ" by leaving the Catholic Church and joining the evangelical group. With tears in his eyes my Catholic brother asked, "Why do you evangelicals do this to us?"

It is no wonder that many priests and bishops are wary of the evangelical missionaries they encounter and view their intentions with suspicion.

Reinforcing the sectarian and "cultist" image of these evangelical groups in the eyes of the receptor society is the activity-centeredness of their approach (Koop 1986:44-46). One example of this style is the attempt to replace Catholic Mass with "worship" in the context of an evangelical style Sunday celebration which is projected as the focal point of the Christian experience. Koop has pointed out that the success of "planting" a small church centered on an evangelical Protestant Sunday celebration, in a place like France, will probably make evangelistic success unlikely (1986:86-87).

The separatist position fails to take seriously the European mentality which links their identity to the church.[7] This is something that North Americans have real difficulty understanding. Although the average Frenchman in the 1990's does not regularly practice his Catholic faith, it is an integral part of his identity. A person is born Catholic or Reformed, and to ask him to give up this heritage is like asking him to give up his nationality:

> Everybody says that they are Catholic—that their roots are Catholic. But today, very few of the Catholics really adhere to their religion. They call themselves "Catholique non-pratiquant"—"I'm a Catholic that doesn't practice my religion." I was baptized a Catholic and I'll die a Catholic, but I don't go to church and I don't necessarily believe in God. (Wilheim 1986:20)

Ecumenical: Kingdom of God/Formal

Those missionaries who find themselves strongly influenced by the kingdom of God paradigm and who are deeply committed to formal, activity-centered ministries would experience the same kind of formalized relationship to the state churches as one sees between the French Reformed Church and the Roman Catholic Church.

Although those in this quadrant acknowledge the other as "truly Christian," there is a distance between "themselves" and the "others" which is measured by important theological differences, the observance of the essential forms of worship, and the various systems of pastoral government. These believers do feel that they can proclaim, together with the state church, the apostolic faith enshrined in the creeds and dogmas of the early church. They can also labor side by side in defending the religious heritage of Christendom in what has become a militantly secularized environment. However, they work to maintain separateness.

These believers do not want to do anything that might be seen as a betrayal of their ecclesiastical heritage enshrined in their religious forms. They worry that if they get too close to other kinds of Christian believers they will be unduly minimizing the theological, doctrinal and ecclesiastical battles fought by their forefathers. They fear that if they don't maintain a certain distance from others they will lose their distinctives.

Separatism does not only concern the missionary population. There are also leaders of the state churches who don't want missionaries crossing over the ecclesiological divide. Several years ago a French bishop urged me to start an evangelical church the way other missionaries do. He was troubled that I had crossed over the gap and entered a ministry of service which did not underline our distinctives and enforce "separateness" from each other.

Sympathetic: Church-Centered/Relational

I have encountered a number of North American evangelical missionaries in France who find themselves in this position. These missionaries are not rigidly hostile toward Catholics, since most French people make little more than a nominal commitment to the Catholic Church. However, although they realize that French Catholics who readily criticize their church are at the same time reluctant to leave it, those in this quadrant believe firmly that it is the presence of regenerate persons that properly constitutes a group as a church (Andersen 1955:15). Some of these missionaries press their converts to sever promptly and completely their connection with Catholicism because of doctrinal differences.

Others in this quadrant take a more temperate approach in an attempt to cooperate with French Catholics who are concerned about the salvation of their friends and neighbors. These missionaries encourage their converts to attend both the missionary group and the state church. This more moderate position usually draws swift rebuke from other missionaries who insist upon doctrinal precision (Koop 1986:147).

As early as twenty years ago, Ramez Atallah, the Quebec Director of InterVarsity Christian Fellowship, pointed out that missionaries ministering under the Indigenous Church Model in post-Christian Roman Catholic lands were facing a severe ministerial dilemma:

> In their present relationships with Roman Catholics, many Protestant missionaries and pastors are facing an acute dilemma. On the one hand, they are enjoying a new and exciting ministry among Catholics through Bible teaching, discussion, prayer and evangelistic activity. On the other hand, this involvement with Catholics is sometimes strongly questioned by the Christian worker's churches or mission boards. The latter are afraid that

such activity by their missionaries may be a compromise of biblical principles.

Many Christian workers caught in this dilemma find it very hard to know what to do. Often, even when they are convinced that their activities do not involve any compromise of biblical principles, they feel forced to either cover up what they do or completely abandon their involvement with Catholics. If they do not do this, many of them face the prospect of losing financial support from their church or mission.

This delicate situation is increasingly becoming the experience of many evangelical Protestants ministering in predominantly Roman Catholic countries. It requires serious, patient, and prayerful consideration by all involved. (1974:881)

Incarnational: Kingdom of God/Relational

The missionaries who find themselves in this quadrant recognize that their mission is to lead men and women to conversion to Christ on the level of their worldview allegiances and commitments. They understand the need to integrate these converts into the Christian community, which they see as a network of mentoring and accountability relationships which are distinguishable from ecclesiastical structures and which transcend denominational distinctives. Their ministry is done life-to-life, unobtrusively, in the intimacy of everyday relationships. They are not concerned about organizing a church or establishing a Christian institution. Their goal is to reconcile people to God without placing undue stumbling blocks in anyone's path (2 Cor. 5:11-6:10).

Furthermore, they believe that they can best proclaim the kingdom of God in post-Christendom lands by assuming the posture of "servants" who "set aside" their own ecclesiastical rights and privileges. They understand that their mission is not to establish a new, distinct, ecclesiastical body of believers or to impose their liturgical forms in these countries marked by centuries of the Church's presence. Rather, they aim to place their unique theological heritage, ministerial experience, and bicultural perspective at the service of the followers of Jesus already present in those lands. In so doing they "become all things to all men," as it were, "in order to win as many as possible" (1 Cor. 9:19-23). Thus the ministry of these missionaries serves to ratify and strengthen the ties of their converts to the Christian church of their own heritage.

Concluding Thoughts

It has been my own observation and experience in France that the closer a North American evangelical ministry finds itself to point "A" in my model, the more it is perceived as culturally inappropriate by the members of French society. Dr J. Herbert Kane, the late Professor Emeritus of the School of World Mission and Evangelism at Trinity Evangelical Divinity School, pointed out that this is a major barrier to our missionary endeavors in Western Europe:

> As far as evangelism among Europeans is concerned, the evangelical missionary has a number of strikes against him, the greatest being their perception of him as an evangelical. They regard us as a cult, just as we regard the Mormons, the Moonies, and the Jehovah's Witnesses. Consequently they will have nothing to do with us. We are there, so they think, to win converts away from their churches and organize them into churches of our own. That, they think, is outright "sheep stealing," and nobody likes that. They will accept us only if they can be persuaded that we are friends, not foes. (1986:2)

We have already seen that French culture is built on mistrust. I believe that it is the way in which the dominant French Catholic subsociety perceives the evangelical Protestant missionary that constitutes the greatest cultural obstacle to the evangelization of France! Koop observes that, unfortunately for us, we are most frequently given the labels that we hope to avoid. All too often we are grouped with the non-Christian sects in the minds of the French.

Moreover, by insisting on the adoption of our North American evangelical Protestant traditions and practices by those with whom we share Christ, we are communicating an unacceptable and non-biblical message to the French. The testimony of Hans Wilheim, a European who presently ministers with Overseas Crusades in Europe, illustrates this point:

> To me, the fact that I, as a German, would feel that I would have to embrace an American-type free church system after having been raised all my life in a Lutheran church setting would be just like requiring an American to say goodbye to apple pie, the American flag, or football. This would be such a radical shift that I wouldn't be willing to do it. (1986:20)

Wilheim continues by asking why we can't do something within the established Church structure:

Over ninety-nine percent of all people have their roots and ties in the state church and I do not see them ever moving out of that. There might be a few moving out here and there. But by and large they are locked into that structure. Why can't we, if we have a national vision for that country, somehow get into that mainstream and see what God will do for us? (1986:20)

On the other hand, my own missionary experience confirms that the closer a North American evangelical ministry is to point "B" in the model, the more contextualized it is to the French situation. Through the years I have endeavored to minister in France from a kingdom of God paradigm stressing relational methods. This has allowed me to accompany more than two hundred French teenagers and adults as they welcomed the Lordship of Christ over their lives. All of these individuals were Catholics. Less than a dozen of these people were practicing their faith when we first met and many said that they were atheists. We accompanied some of these men and women in their spiritual pilgrimage for several months, others for more than a decade.

It has been fairly common to hear one or another of these individuals testify that they "rediscovered" their church after I helped them to ratify their baptism by acknowledging Jesus as their Lord and Savior. To my knowledge no one has left the Catholic Church because of my involvement in their life.

A good number of these people are actively accompanying their neighbors and friends in their spiritual pilgrimage; some have taken places of leadership in their parishes. It is interesting that these believers are sometimes accused of taking Jesus too seriously because they have moved from nominality to a vital relationship with Jesus Christ. They are not seen as being "cultist"; instead, they are perceived as "Catholics who are not quite like the others."

Evangelizing and discipling French people in the context of human relationships, without forming them into a visible entity which exists outside of or alongside the state church, enables them to remain in vital contact with neighbors, friends and family members who would otherwise consider them members of a strange cult. The result is that rather than becoming a small, ingrown group of believers, the missionary, and the French believers who have been influenced for Christ, have an ever-widening web of ministry relationships in the communities where they live.

Notes

1. (p. 56) J. I. Packer gives the following description of the kingdom of God (1995:166):

   > The kingdom of God exists wherever Christ reigns as king and God's revealed will is actually done. The life of the faithful disciple is the kingdom—that is, the rule of Christ—in individual manifestation; the life of the faithful congregation is the kingdom in corporate manifestation; the life of a faithful parachurch body is the kingdom in a form of executive manifestation, inasmuch as all the doings of such a body aim to be kingdom activities, gestures of obedience to Christ that express and extend his rule over human lives.

2. (p. 56) This is, in my opinion, the major difference between the two missional paradigms. The church-centered model encourages individual groups of believers to assert and develop themselves as Beyerhaus has noted (1979:26): "The danger inherent in the individual's assertion of self also threatens the Church. It is possible for a church to affirm its human 'self' against God, and so to become odious to both God and man. The Church should therefore hesitate to apply to itself an ideal that stresses the affirmation of the self."

3. (p. 56) Hoekendijk used the term "Churchification" to identify the way in which evangelism is often corrupted to mean the extension of the numbers, influence and prestige of the church under the church-centered paradigm (1950:134). He contended that "Church-centric thinking" is bound to go astray because it revolves around what he labeled an "illegitimate center":

   > When results are considered, it seems to make little difference whether independent, indigenous Churches, or popular or national Churches rooted in the soil, or the ecumenical world Church is regarded as the goal of missionary endeavor; in every case, wherever the missionary enterprise is dominated by a Church-centric conception, that is bound in the long run to end by imperiling its very existence. (cited in Andersen 1955:39)

4. (p. 56) I am not advocating here some sort of diffuse blessing called "the Kingdom of God" in opposition to the Church. Nor am I using the kingdom of God paradigm to indicate some sort of human utopia, perfect fellowship, or spiritual identification with the values of justice, truth, joy and love. Instead, I am suggesting that we must adopt an approach that discerns the interrelation of the local church and the kingdom of God. Furthermore, I am suggesting that the establishing of local churches cannot be an end in itself. This position seems to be in line with that of the evangelical theologian of missions, Charles Van Engen, who has brilliantly argued that the Church is not the final goal of mission (1993:111). Following the thinking of Avery Dulles,

Van Engen writes:

> Because the kingdom is more inclusive, more extensive, more perfect, and more comprehensive than the Church, the Church must be understood as the servant of the kingdom. Precisely in this service the Church becomes uniquely meaningful (1993·113)

My experience has been that missionaries working in France under the paradigmatic ideal of the "church-centric" model experience unnecessary difficulty in knowing how to relate to members of other Christian churches. I am suggesting that a proper understanding of God's kingly rule, and a recognition that the churches are servants of His kingdom, will free us to do away with denominational affiliations and institutional structures that inhibit our witness to Jesus as the Christ and King in post-Christendom lands.

5. (p. 56) I do not contrast this term with "informal." Rather, I place it in contrast to "relational." I use "formal" to denote the typical activist mindset and missionary outlook of English-speaking evangelicalism which tends to formalize relationships. In this perspective, following Jesus and "being the Church" are understood as things that one does (either individually or in community with others) rather than living relationships.

6. (p. 62) Reinforcing the Pietist "individualism" was the thesis which gained widespread acceptance among conservative missionaries after World War I, that the Scriptures clearly taught the obligation to separate from those with whom one disagreed. Hence the evangelical believers, who had developed a strong antipathy toward the views of other Protestants and toward Roman Catholicism in general and who found little indication that other Christians should be considered part of the Church in any way, sought to establish indigenous churches of "sound faith."

7. (p. 63) For a detailed description of this phenomenon see J. Edward Boon (1982:15).

Chapter 6

Let This Mind Be in You ...

About now you are probably wondering what I actually do in my ministry among the French and how I spend my time. You might ask: "If your emphasis is not on church activities, if you don't have a centralized gathering of those individuals you are accompanying in the faith, then is your ministry structureless? How can you ever tell if you are accomplishing anything? Is it possible to measure the results of the kind of ministry that you labeled "incarnational" in the last chapter? Where do ministry goals and accountability to your donors fit into the picture?"

These are all very important questions! However, before I enter into an explanation of the details of our ministry to the French, I find it important to state once again that I am not pleading in favor of yet another method of "church planting" or a new church growth strategy. Instead, I am calling for a reexamination of missionary spirituality. It is my conviction that it is our spirituality, not our sociology or anthropology, that should give birth to and establish the limits of our ministry. Without the proper spirituality our ministry might reflect a correct understanding of the dynamics of human interaction in society but it will not display an appropriate understanding of how God has drawn near to mankind.

One of the fundamental lessons to be learned from the Incarnation is that the messenger is the message. Jesus of Nazareth did not simply "give" us a message from God: He *was* the message from God. Jesus claimed that people could not receive or understand His testimony unless they received Him (John 8:42-47). In Jesus the message and the messenger are indistinguishable. He is the divine Word! In like manner Christ's witnesses are intimately and inextricably the message they deliver to the world. It is because we not only have a message and ministry from God to the world, but also are the message and ministry of God in the world that we must cultivate the proper spirituality.

Developing a Missionary Spirituality from the Kenosis

Whenever the followers of Jesus have reflected on the mystery of the Incarnation they have interpreted it as an act of divine self-emptying or limitation. What has mystified and astonished Christ's followers for nearly two thousand years is Jesus' willingness to set aside His divine privilege and status for our salvation. Throughout the ages men and women have marveled that the eternal pre-existent Logos would reduce Himself as He did to the rank and measure of humanity. In the mystery of the Incarnation, God, through an act of self-emptying called *kenosis* [1] brought about the reality of Immanuel—God with us (Matt. 1:22).

From the earliest formulations of the kenosis theme in the New Testament it is clear that belief in the divine self-emptying is not an isolated affirmation of Christian faith. The kenosis is the biblical answer to the question: "How does God redeem the world?" The affirmation found at the very heart of the Christian faith is that in Jesus Christ, God has freely and totally given Himself (Dawe 1963:20). The divine kenosis is the key to the whole drama of human salvation.

My purpose here is not to trace the various streams of kenotic teaching in the New Testament or church history (for this information see Bruce 1955, Dawe 1963, Richard 1982 and Erickson 1991). I purpose simply to demonstrate that the kenosis gives us invaluable insight into missionary spirituality.

Lessons from Philippians 2:5-7

Learn to see things from other people's point of view. Let Christ Jesus be your example as to what your attitude should be. For he, who had always been God by nature, did not cling to his prerogatives as God's equal, but stripped himself of all privilege ...

J. B. Phillips, *The New Testament in Modern English* (London: Geoffrey Bles, 1960)

The attitude you should have is one that Christ Jesus had: he always had the nature of God, but he did not think that by force he should try to become equal with God. Instead of this, of his own

free will he gave up all he had, and took the nature of a servant ...
Good News Bible, 4th edition (New York: American Bible Society, 1976)

Let your bearing towards one another arise out of your life in Christ Jesus. For the divine nature was his from the first; yet he did not think to snatch at equality with God, but made himself nothing, assuming the nature of a slave ...
New English Bible (New York: Cambridge University Press, 1971)

Your attitude should be the same that Jesus Christ had. Though he was God, he did not demand and cling to his rights as God. He made himself nothing, he took the humble position of a slave ...
New Living Translation (Wheaton, IL: Tyndale House Publishers, 1996)

What strikes me as I reread these verses is that they describe the kenosis as something very concrete and active. Jesus didn't just think about humbling Himself. He didn't simply give Himself the label "servant." These verses say that He "made himself nothing," He "stripped himself of all privilege," He "took the humble position of a slave." Wow! Jesus actively stepped down from His place of power, and became a servant on our behalf. He didn't wait for someone else to do this to Him; He did it to Himself.

Jesus told His followers that they should follow His example in humble service (John 13:15) and that the greatest among them would be those who made themselves the servants of all (Mark 9:35).

Most of us like to be thought of as servants; few of us like to be treated like servants! In these verses from Philippians, the Apostle Paul uses the appeal to Christ's self-emptying as the basis for an admonition to humility and service. Paul holds before the Philippian congregation Christ's supreme example of humility in leaving the heavenly realm to "dwell in the form of a servant." Similarly, in 2 Corinthians the theme of Christ's kenosis is used as the basis of an appeal for liberality in giving to the poor of the Jerusalem church (2 Cor. 8:9). In both of these contexts the appeal to the kenosis is both practical and active.

I submit for your reflection, three principles for the development of a missionary spirituality based on the divine kenosis. These principles inform a kenotic missiology which, I believe, enlightens and makes intelligible the role of the evangelical Protestant missionary in post-Christendom lands.

PRINCIPLE I. The kenosis is not only a descriptive of the Servant Lord, but it involves the servant people. It describes the quality of the life of faith and obedience of the disciple of Christ. The moral appeal of God's free self-giving is the motivation for the life of self-giving love for the follower of Christ.

All followers of Christ, everywhere, are constrained by the example of their Lord to give themselves freely for others. Rank and status often keep us from giving ourselves to others. It is often our attainments that distance us from those Christ calls us to serve. Each rung of the corporate ladder widens the gap between the worker and the management. Each diploma hanging on the wall separates the professor from the student. Each Olympic medal or championship ring or title lifts the exceptional athlete out of the realm of mere human accomplishment. In like manner, each of our religious attainments and each of our theological "certainties" has the potential to separate us from those we are called to accompany in the faith!

Paul apparently understood this, for he claimed that to the "weak" he became "weak" so as to "win the weak" (1 Cor. 9:22). Paul did not minister to the weak from a position of strength! He did not allow his attainments to separate him from those Christ had sent him to serve. In fact, Paul claims that although he was "free" he willingly and freely followed the example of Christ Who gave up His divine rights, privileges, and prerogatives, by making Himself a servant of all (1 Cor. 9:19).

Evangelical Protestant missionaries ministering in post-Christendom lands have a number of prerogatives, rights and privileges that they must be willing to abandon if they would enter into incarnational service to the people of God already present in those places. I believe that we must be willing to strip ourselves of the "right" to be seen as the equals of the clergy of the churches of historic Christendom (some of those churches do not recognize the legitimacy of our ordination). We must rid ourselves of the "privilege" of preaching the Word of God from the pulpit each Sunday. We must abandon the prerogatives of those who minister in a highly visible, liturgical and sacramental way. We must give up our right to celebrate the Lord's Supper, to baptize, to marry, to bury.

In the same manner, the mission sending agency must be willing to abandon its right to expect its own kind of churches to be produced by the ministry it supports. Whereas in my own case the Missionary Church has always sent Missionary Church missionaries to "plant" Missionary Church churches, this should no longer be the expectation. The mission agency must strip itself of the right to extend itself overseas.

Parachurch organizations like Campus Crusade for Christ, InterVarsity Christian Fellowship, Young Life, and Overseas Crusades seem to find it easier to strip themselves of this prerogative and enter into a ministry of service to the existing church in post-Christendom lands. Denominational missions and Independent church-planting missions would do well to follow their example.

PRINCIPLE II. The kenosis answers the question how God can both empty Himself and remain unchanged.

The kenosis reminds us that although God became man and a servant, He remained God. I have read a number of testimonies of evangelical Protestant leaders who have recently converted to Roman Catholicism. This, I believe, is not the appropriate answer to missions in post-Christendom lands. Most of those who are converting from one Christian faith community to another are pursuing the goal of being a part of the "most perfect or complete" church. As one former evangelical Protestant missionary to Guatemala wrote (Franklin 1996:36): "In the Catholic Church we have found the fullness of the Christian faith. Not seventy-five percent of the Truth, not ninety-percent, but all of it, one hundred percent." How unfortunate the person has come to this conclusion!

I don't think that God is asking us to attempt to discern which group of believers has the most perfect understanding of Jesus' message and the most complete understanding of what it means to be His follower. In fact, I find it quite arrogant to think that I am able to see and discern more clearly than the members of the groups that I reject as "inferior" brands of Christianity. Perhaps our judgment in these cases is more a reflection of our own personalities, spiritual sensitivities and life experiences than it is an objective appraisal of the validity of any given Christian experience or expression.

The question that I must ask, as a missionary in a post-Christendom land, is not what faith community has the most truth! The question that must preoccupy my thoughts is: "How can I bring the light which I have received from my own faith tradition and religious heritage and serve the followers of Jesus in this place?" Such an attitude of humility and selflessness enables the missionary to learn with and from those he or she is called to accompany in the faith. None of us have arrived at a complete understanding of God's self-revelation. No single faith community has appropriated all of God's truth. We are all pilgrims. We are all in process. And we need each other.

As an evangelical Protestant missionary working in the midst of the Roman Catholic subsociety of the French world, I have certain things both to offer to and learn from that faith community. This two-way communication, this partnership in ministry, is facilitated as we come in the Spirit of the Servant Christ.

PRINCIPLE III. In the light of the kenosis we understand that God does not redeem by overpowering might or by a sheer unveiling of His glory. In stark opposition to all human attempts at salvation by self-assertions, the characteristic saving act of God is one of self-emptying.

Erickson suggests that in the kenosis Jesus did not give up the qualities of God, but He gave up the privilege of exercising them, so he proposes that Philippians 2:7 should be translated: "He emptied Himself by taking the form of a servant" (1991:555). Isn't this a fascinating concept? When we assume the role of a servant to the historic churches in Christendom lands we are not really giving up anything. I have found that by limiting my freedom in certain areas of my ministry to the French, God has opened up entirely new and exciting avenues of service which had previously been closed to me.

A General Overview of the Needs in France

The kenosis tells us that in Jesus of Nazareth the divine took the form of a servant. Servants exist to serve and to meet needs. When God broke into my world back in 1979 and revealed to me that He has a people in the Catholic Church, one of my first reactions was, "Then why did you lead me here? What are the needs experienced by Your people in this place that You want to meet through the unique equipping and preparation that You have given to me via my own spiritual heritage?" As I have meditated on these questions, three broad areas of spiritual need have come to my attention.

The Need for Effective Evangelism

As we noted in chapter 4, most of the American evangelical Protestant missionaries working in France admit that the results of their evangelistic efforts are slim. After more than fifty years of intense North American evangelical Protestant missionary activity in France, there are evangelical missionaries firmly planted in practically every region. There are church buildings scattered up and down the land with hundreds of "strategic centers," several Bible schools, and a great corps of dedicated missionaries and a company of national fellow workers. There are Christian publishing houses which distribute their literature in France, gospel radio broadcasts emanating from Monté Carlo, and Christian television programs aired on Sunday mornings. It is difficult to imagine a more strategic disposition of resources. Despite this favorable set-up, however, the evangelization of France is not proceeding as it should. After almost fifty-five years of modern evangelical Protestant missionary endeavors in France, less than one fourth of one percent of the French are evangelical Protestants. [2] The strategies for the evangelization of the French used by this missionary force clearly need to be reevaluated. The evangelical Protestant missionaries will not significantly influence the French for Christ by simply continuing to energetically and devoutly carry on their "mission work."

Even the Roman Catholic Church has experienced difficulties in her attempts to proclaim the gospel to the French. As early as 1951 the World Council of Churches published a report stating that, "A complete picture of religious vitality in France would show that at least four-fifths of the population have no contact whatsoever with the Christian Church, and live in total ignorance of the gospel" (1951:2).

One reason why the believing Catholics have difficulty leading their friends and neighbors to faith in Christ is because they are so closely associated with the religious structures of the Catholic faith. Most of the French reject the institutional church and are ignorant of the person and teaching of Christ.

A second reason why our Roman Catholic brothers, be they priests or practicing laypeople, have a problem communicating the gospel in France is their vocabulary. Many of these believers only know how to explain the gospel in the terms given them by their Catholic tradition, and most of the French are deaf to that terminology. In other words, they often lack the biblical knowledge and vocabulary which we evangelical Protestants possess and utilize in evangelization.

If you were to approach the priest with whom I prayed for three and a half years with the following question: "Father, I sense the presence of God's Spirit in your life. How can I enter into the same kind of relationship with God that you experience?" do you know what he would say? This dear brother would probably say something like: "Keep praying. Keep looking. Keep attending Mass." In all of Father X's praying, searching for God and communing at the Eucharist he has entered into a very real and active relationship with God the Father. I guess that we evangelical Protestant missionaries would say that he "stumbled onto a real relationship with God." It is probably more accurate to say that he was brought to make the appropriate personal commitments of his life to Christ through the faith of the believing community which surrounded him and by the liturgy and sacraments of the church. The only problem is that the majority of the French do not experience this kind of dynamic interaction with the church. Father X doesn't really have the necessary tools or experience to reach these people who are "Catholic atheists."

The Need for Christian Communities

Another basic need which has been identified as existing in France is the need to develop communities of faith where people learn together how to live as followers of Jesus. Stephen Clark, a leading Roman Catholic layman, expressed the need for vital communities of faith in these words:

> Here is a major problem which the Church faces. A Christian must have an environment in his life in which Christianity is openly accepted, talked about and lived if he is going to live a very vital Christian life. If he does not have this, his whole life as a Christian will be weak and might even die away. Yet fewer and fewer Catholics are finding such an environment. (1972:40)

In recent years, through the impetus of the Catholic charismatics, we have witnessed the birth of highly visible, tightly structured communities in response to this need. These communities encourage religious vocations, aiding needy families, hosting retreats, working with youth, and street witnessing. These communities involve the members in a deep commitment with the Lord and other brothers and sisters that transcends parish jurisdiction (Ward 1997, Lenoir 1988, Hébrard 1987, Leclerc 1986).

I do not believe that it is enough to simply bring individual Frenchmen to a place of repentance and personal allegiance to Christ. It is also necessary for their growth to spiritual maturity that we provide an environment, a community of believers, where they can learn with others how to handle the issues of life in a Christ-like way. It is in such a community that the convert is nurtured, because the members of such a community learn to take careful note of each other's spiritual, social, mental, and physical welfare and development (Heb.10:24-25).

Jesus Christ said to His disciples in Matthew chapter 9 that the harvest is plentiful but that the workers are few. This is certainly true of France today. Jesus also told His disciples that one of their *raisons d'être* was the discipling of the peoples of the world (Matt. 28:19). According to Ephesians 4:11, God's plan is to bring the believers to spiritual maturity. This plan includes, along with the work of the Holy Spirit, human instruments also: "It was He who gave some to be apostles, some to be prophets, some to be evangelists, and some to be pastors and teachers." This brings us to recognize a third major need facing the Christian church in France: where will these "gifted men" who are to equip the saints come from?

The Need for Laborers and Leaders

Laborers and leaders are a very real need in France at the present time. There are actually about 600 North American evangelical Protestant missionaries in France, of whom approximately 450 are in active service at any one time. Can we count on these missionaries to reach the 57 million French people and then build them to maturity in Christ? Evans, in response to this question, has stated: "If we depend on the missionaries, we'll never win France. We are not numerous enough. It has been said that the missionaries are expensive, inefficient and temporary. We need to create a French witnessing group" (quoted in Smeeton 1980:216).

It is my conviction that it is best that the leadership within the nurturing communities to which we give birth be "natural" or "emergent" leadership. This is to say that we have found that through the process of discipling our converts, certain individuals have emerged as "naturals" to fulfill certain functions within those communities. These are the Spirit-gifted individuals that God promised to give to His church to guide His people to maturity. The leaders come from the ranks of the disciples. For this reason we feel that a person must "grow into the ministry, rather than go into the ministry"! As the giftedness and moral character of these people is acknowledged and affirmed by the faith community, they receive training to equip them to lead.

We Preach Not Ourselves, But Christ Jesus the Lord, and Ourselves Your Servants for Jesus' Sake

So how do we go about meeting some of these needs? In our examination of French culture we saw the importance of adapting our lifestyle and ministry methods in order to avoid creating unnecessary barriers for the people who would be converted. This is part of the genius of the Scriptures and the work of the Holy Spirit. They set people free to approach each new situation differently and to minister in Jesus' name in any culture and at any time in history. I borrow the following example from Gene Getz to illustrate this truth:

> Whether you study the structure of Peter's sermons, or follow Paul as he moved out from the Jewish community into the Gentile world, one thing is certain! These men were not locked into one approach or a single way of presenting the divine message. They varied their methodology, depending on the circumstances. (1974:48)

Getz continues by stating why, in his opinion, we are sometimes slow to emulate the missionary example of Peter and Paul:

> One of the key problems with the evangelical church in the twentieth century is that we have allowed non-absolutes to become absolute. We have permitted "ways of doing things" to become normative.
>
> On the one hand we have taken biblical patterns (which vary considerably throughout the Bible) and fixate on the one we feel is the right one; perhaps the one with which we feel the most comfortable. Rather than viewing all biblical examples as divine resources which yield absolute principles and guidelines, we develop tunnel vision and allow ourselves to get locked into a single method.
>
> Furthermore, we have allowed purely human patterns and forms which have been developed in the last fifty to one hundred years to become absolute. We actually believe some of the ways we do things now are biblical norms. (1974:48-49)

Certain adaptations to French culture are obvious. For example, we must speak French, and adopt French costume and grooming, housing, dietary patterns, sports, celebrations, etc. All of these adaptations must be made without compromising biblical principles. But when we come to methodology for ministry it is more difficult for us to discern those things that are absolutes and those that can be changed so as to be appropriate within the receptor culture. Getz reminds us that we have the tendency to absolutize the use of various forms of ministry.

It is not wrong to use methods in ministry that have proved helpful in the past. What *is* wrong is to get so locked into a "way" of ministering in Christ's name that we are unwilling to strip ourselves of certain roles and activities that actually keep us from effectively reaching people for Christ in our new context. What makes it doubly wrong is when we classify our methods as a biblical norm. We need to be free to allow the Spirit of God to lead us into new ways of accompanying people in the faith and free to rid ourselves of old and counter-productive forms and structures.

The Importance of Relationships

St. Luke's Gospel insists that Jesus was continually involved "seeking and saving the lost" (Luke 19:10). This is given as the driving force in Jesus' life, His all-consuming passion (see Luke 4:18-19). What fascinates me about Luke's account of the life of Christ is that this ministry of seeking and saving the lost is seen in the light of personal relationships, intimate conversations and one-on-one encounters. In Luke's Gospel we see Jesus reaching out to redeem mankind one lost person at a time!

Jesus' encounter with the tax collector Zacchaeus amply illustrates this point. Imagine the scene as Luke describes it in chapter 19 of his Gospel. Jesus, passing through Jericho, has drawn a large crowd and Zacchaeus, being a short man, could not see him. "So," Luke writes, "he ran ahead and climbed a sycamore-fig tree to see him, since Jesus was coming that way" (Luke 19:4).

Now, what would you or I do in this kind of situation? Were we in Jesus' place we would probably set up a microphone and preach the gospel message to the crowd. Perhaps we would have the multitude break up into smaller groups which we would assign to the care of the disciples so that they could communicate the message more clearly. Some of us would want to make sure that each person received a piece of gospel literature. We would want to minister to as many as possible, as quickly as possible.

But Jesus did not do any of these things! Jesus looked beyond the crowd and saw one man "up a tree." Jesus walked through a crowd of interested "seekers" and zeroed in on one individual. This is a pattern that we see throughout the ministry of Christ. Jesus seemed to value depth of ministry over scope of ministry.

Chapter 7 will describe the ways in which we seek to accompany the French in their walk of faith. The process I will describe is given to illustrate one possible way of applying the principles outlined in these pages. This process demonstrates the priority that I give to relationship-based ministry over activity-based outreach. This process does not present a "methodology" for ministry in post-Christendom lands! It is offered in the hope that it will "flesh out" some of the implications of an incarnational approach to the missionary enterprise.

Notes

1. (p. 71) Kenosis is a theme expressed through Christian literature in every age. From the early Christian hymn in Philippians to a sermon by Origen, from a treatise of Tertullian to the hymns of Wesley, from the homilies of Gregory of Nazianzus to the meditations of Zinzendorf, from the mystical writings of Bernard to the ontology of Hegel, from the sermons of Luther to the theology of Barth, the kenosis motif is found. However, consideration of the kenosis has usually been limited to New Testament studies or, at most, extended to cover the so-called kenotic Christologies formulated during the nineteenth and early twentieth centuries. Whenever the kenosis idea is mentioned, the names of Gottfried Thomasius (1965:46), Bishop Gore (1889:299-302), or P. T. Forsyth (1909:183-224), and others come to mind. These men attempted to build a modern Christology on the basis of the kenosis motif. Although the Christologies developed by these men have come under sharp criticism I do not think that the kenosis doctrine is passé, or should be relegated to a corner in New Testament history. I believe that the kenosis is not simply a matter of certain Christologies formulated by theologians of the past. Rather, I find it central to the faith of the church and the heart of appropriate missiological spirituality.

2. (p. 76) During the Anglo-Saxon Intermissions Study Conference held at the Château de St. Albain, March 16-18, 1981, the following pertinent statistics were given: of a population of 54 million Frenchmen, 250,000 are Protestants. Ives Perrier, the General Secretary of the French Evangelical Alliance estimated at that time that of these, 128,000 were evangelical Protestants (maximum), of whom one-half are Pentecostals. That makes 0.22 percent of the French population evangelical Protestants. (Taken from the minutes of the Field Council of the "Mission Evangélique des Alpes Françaises," March 27, 1981.)

Chapter 7

An Alternative Approach to Missions in Post-Christendom Lands

How can we effectively introduce French men and women to Jesus Christ? Is it possible to give birth to communities of faith in France that are characterized by New Testament life and vitality? To what extent are we to allow the spiritual, cultural and historical realities that we have dealt with in this book to shape our approach to ministry in France? What follows is a description of some of the concrete ways in which we have structured our ministry in answer to these questions.

Evangelism

We had been living in our rented home on the outskirts of Caen for a couple of years when one Saturday afternoon we noticed people visiting the empty barn next door. Because we had never met these people, we decided to go over and see if we could be of some help.

After we met the young couple and their two small children, they invited us to join them as they toured the barn (in which they planned to open a family business) and the small living quarters that had been built into the front of the structure. After we visited the place with this couple and talked for some time, they informed us that they had decided to begin renting this barn immediately. The following week they moved in and got set up in their new living quarters.

During our tour of the small apartment with this couple Diane and I noticed that although the building had two bedrooms, a living room, kitchen and water closet, it had no bathroom. There was no place for this family of four to take a bath or shower. So, after prayer and discussion together, we decided that we should put in a bathroom for this family.

Remember, we had just met this couple. They did not ask us to do this job. They didn't even know that we had discussed their need when I showed up on Monday morning with a missionary colleague to begin the work.

For the next two weeks I labored to add a room to this family's apartment. I didn't ask them to pay for the materials. I didn't ask for their help. Day after day I worked putting up walls, running copper tubes, installing fixtures, hanging doors, painting, laying tile.

As I was grouting floor-tiles one afternoon, the young woman's father, who was visiting from out of town, laid his hand on my shoulder and said: "You must be really a nice guy to be doing all this for my daughter and her family!"

To which I responded, "Not at all! I am not doing this because I am a nice guy! I am doing this because if Jesus of Nazareth moved in here I would want Him to have a shower and sink." This large man nearly fell to the floor in shock! He had imagined a lot of explanations for my service, but never had Jesus entered into the equation.

Over the next weeks and months Diane and I got to know this young family. We spent evenings together playing cards and talking. The wife taught Diane how to prepare some French dishes, and the husband and I played tennis together. We learned the details of their lives, the broken relationships they had experienced, their joys and pains, their reasons for hope or despair. As they watched how we related to our children and to each other, as they witnessed how we handled the pressures of daily living, they became increasingly trusting and open.

About six months later, after many animated discussions, this non-practicing, Catholic atheist couple came to faith in Christ. They came to appreciate (in our living room) what we knew about Jesus only after they had learned (in their bathroom) how much we cared about them. Today this Catholic couple is actively involved in their diocese introducing young people to Christ.

This testimony illustrates something that I have repeatedly observed. While French culture is not unlike North American culture in many aspects, the history of recent evangelistic endeavors in France reveals that the French are much more receptive to personal, relationship-based witness for Christ than they are to evangelistic campaigns or crusades.

It is also important that we avoid snatching individuals out of their Catholic social setting and placing them into an evangelical Protestant group on their conversion. Evangelism entails the proclamation of the historical, biblical Christ as Savior and Lord, with a view to persuading people to come to Him personally and so be reconciled to God. Coming to Jesus Christ means pledging to Him allegiance and obedience.

> I define a convert as one who, with repentance and faith, has turned away from sin and self and has turned toward God (Acts 3:19). The convert has made a public confession that he/she no longer lives for himself but for Jesus Christ (Rom. 14:8-9; 2 Cor. 5:15-17; Rom. 12:1-2; Luke 9:23; Rom. 10:9-10).

Table 7-1 Profile of a Convert

Conversion does not necessarily mean changing one's religious identity![1] In fact, I contend that the process of extracting individuals from their setting in Catholic society retards their own growth in the faith and hinders the expansion of the kingdom of God. Contemporary history shows that it rouses antagonism against evangelical Protestantism and produces many unfortunate and sometimes tragic results in the lives of those most deeply concerned. It deprives the converts of the support and encouragement of their families and friends, brands them as heretics, and creates walls of suspicion which hamper their testimony for Christ, and sacrifices much of the convert's evangelistic potential. When conversion to Christ results in a change of religious identity or affiliation of this kind, it often produces anemic churches that know little of indigenous leadership and are held together chiefly by common dependence on the mission or the missionary (Olsen 1977).

It is equally obvious that the evangelization of the French people requires true conversion. Hence we see our task as that of leading French men and women to a point of repentance and new life commitments and allegiances through the communication of the gospel. To do this we invite our interested neighbors and friends to join us in small Bible discussion groups. These groups meet weekly in homes. We have found that it takes from three months to one year of regularly looking at the person and teachings of Jesus in the Gospels before he or she will come to the place of commitment of his or her life to Christ. We have found that the best evangelistic approach is to present the gospel in this straightforward way. Our responsibility as missionary-evangelists is to make the Gospel of Christ as clear and compelling as possible.

Another very important aspect in conversion is the renouncing of past sin and the breaking of spiritual strongholds in the life of the would-be follower of Jesus. Even in the case of individuals where there is no apparent demonization, I have found it important to lead the person through a process of spiritual inner cleansing at the time of conversion. Intergenerational spiritual power must be broken and all curses must be replaced with blessing. Any involvement with occultic spirituality must be totally renounced. Most importantly, the new convert must be led through a period of forgiving the past offenses and hurts of others at the same time that he or she receives the forgiveness of Christ.

Establishing the Converts

Dr. Howard Hendricks, professor of Christian Education at Dallas Theological Seminary, in the foreword of the book, *Disciples Are Made— Not Born*, states: "Make disciples is the mandate of the Master (Matt. 28:19-20). We may ignore it, but we cannot evade it" (Henrichsen 1974:5). Veteran missionary to Europe, Bob Evans, has this to say about the need to disciple converts to Christ:

> We must train the nationals. Discipleship both inside and especially outside the institution should be taking place on all levels. The question to be asked of the missionary is, "Where are your disciples?" To the extent that they are saved, motivated and trained, to that extent we are successful. (Smeeton 1980:216)

The Great Commission of our Lord is quite emphatic about the importance of teaching new believers the Word of God. "Make disciples," exhorted Jesus, and then "teach" these disciples. You cannot make disciples if you do not teach them the truths of God's Word.

And this is what the Apostles did, for the new believers in Jerusalem were "continually devoting themselves to the apostles' teaching ..." (Acts 2:42). There was the immediate intake of biblical truth and doctrine. "Like newborn babes," wrote Peter, "crave pure spiritual milk, so that by it you may grow up in your salvation" (1 Peter 2:2).

No one can deny the importance of solid biblical teaching in the process of edification. Any mission or ministry of the church that does not provide good biblical instruction does not follow the New Testament pattern.[2] It is important to note, however, that the form that this teaching took varied greatly. There are no absolute guidelines or stereotyped patterns. The methods and approaches—whether used by

Jesus, the Apostles, or other members of the faith community—varied according to situation. Sometimes the group was large; sometimes it was small. Sometimes the teaching was done by one person; other times it was done by two or more. Sometimes the presentation was lengthy; sometimes it was brief. Sometimes it took place spontaneously; at other times it was planned. Sometimes it was basically a lecture; more often, however, it involved the people in interaction and discussion. Sometimes it was verbalized; sometimes it was visualized. Sometimes it involved mostly transmission of the truth; sometimes it involved a process. But all methods had one objective in view among the followers of Christ: their growth and edification. The methods and approaches were simply means to this important end.

It is also important to observe that the New Testament does not offer us one pattern for the sequence in which biblical truths are to be taught to the new convert. It seems obvious to me that the new follower of Christ must progress from instruction in "basic doctrine" to an ever-growing deeper knowledge of God's truth. David Hesselgrave points out the necessity for discerning between what truths must be taught immediately to the new convert and those that can be learned at a later date:

> Jesus told his disciples to teach "all things whatsoever I have commanded you" (Matthew 28:20, KJV). Paul closely followed this instruction. He wrote, "For I received from the Lord that which I also delivered to you" (I Corinthians 11:23). Timothy was exhorted to teach faithful men so that they in turn could teach others (II Timothy 2:2). Teaching the Word of God to believers is just as imperative for us as it was for Paul and Timothy!
>
> It is obvious, however, that the "all things" must be taught in a space-time context. Not everything can be taught or learned at once. This fact makes the question of priorities important. What truths or practices are so important that they must be taught early in the Christian life? (1982:305-306)

The Apostle Paul gave the following instructions to the followers of Christ living in Colosse: "So then, just as you received Christ Jesus as Lord, continue to live in him, rooted and built up in him, strengthened in the faith as you were taught, and overflowing with thankfulness" (Col. 2:6-7). I call this process of "strengthening in the faith," follow-up. It is here that I begin with the new converts. I help them to discover what the Bible and the church teach about the following areas of the Christian life:

The supremacy of Christ	Col. 1:15-23
The believer's new identity in Christ	Col. 2:8-15
The place of the Scriptures	Col. 3:16
The need for holy living	Col. 3:5-14
The necessity of prayer	Col. 4:2-4
The need for the Family of God	Col. 3:15
The need for worship	Col. 3:16-17
The need to witness to Christ	Col. 4:5-6

This instruction is given within the context of the small Bible discussion "cell groups" and in one-on-one encounters. While some of this instruction is formal, much of it is done informally, around a shared meal, during a trip, or sitting in front of an open fireplace on a winter's evening. It is a sort of apprenticeship in that it focuses on the "how to's" as much as the "why's" of these areas of Christian experience (Clinton & Clinton 1991, Hendricks 1995). For example, I show these young believers how to spend time each day "sitting at the feet of Jesus and learning from him" (Luke 10:39). I teach them how to memorize and meditate on the Scriptures. I introduce them to a simple method of inductive Bible study. I help them to formulate the testimony of what Christ has done in their lives in a clear and concise manner. At this point in the individual's new spiritual development I am more concerned with formation than with information.

Please don't misunderstand me. Giving information is good, but at least at this point in the young convert's development, it is the least effective way of helping him or her to develop spiritually. So rather than spending a lot of time teaching the new convert that he or she should pray, for example, I spend a lot of time praying with them. Instead of simply exhorting them to begin worshipping with other believers, I accompany them to Mass. Instead of doing a Bible study on the need to witness, I provide them with low-risk opportunities to share their faith with others.

This continual mixing of informal teaching and practical application seems to be the method that Jesus Christ used in His ministry. You never see Him leading His disciples in a verse-by-verse analysis of the Torah. I have a difficult time imagining Him saying, "Well, don't forget that tomorrow morning we'll be having devotions from eight to nine. From nine to ten we'll have the minor prophets. Then from ten to eleven we'll have poetry books, and then from eleven to noon we will have homiletics and hermeneutics." Yet He was preparing the best ministers history has ever seen. How could He overlook so many important topics?

A disciple is one who willfully places himself or herself under the Lordship and authority of Jesus Christ each day of his or her life. The disciple lives with the realization that once he or she lived under the power and authority of Satan, but now has been made a bond-slave of Christ (Luke 6:40; 9:23; Rom. 6:3,4).

A disciple is one who has a consistent intake of God's Word and who is bringing thought patterns (through meditation) and lifestyle (through obedience) into conformity to God's Word (John 8:31,32; Phil. 4:8-9; John 14:21).

A disciple is one who continues to seek the Lord earnestly. He or she is cultivating an intimate relationship with God through consistent, daily time spent alone with Christ, incorporating Bible reading, prayer and meditation (Jer. 29:13; Mark 1:35; Psalm 42:1,2).

A disciple is one who is growing in his or her communication with God on behalf of himself or herself and the world. The disciple is convinced of the truth that God shapes the world through our prayers and he or she is experiencing God's answers to his or her prayers (John 14:13,14; 15:7; 16:23,24; Phil. 4:6,7).

A disciple is one who is growing in Christ-like love as demonstrated by sacrificial serving and giving (Phil. 2:3-8; James 2:14-17; Isa. 58:6-12).

A disciple is one who is committed to the other members of Christ's Body, the Church. He or she is one who, in love, takes careful note of the others' spiritual, social, mental and physical welfare and development (Heb. 10:24,25; Phil. 2:3,4; John 13:34,35).

A disciple is one who believes that Jesus Christ is present and actively working toward the salvation of humanity in His church. The disciple understands that the sacraments which are part of the life of the church were instituted by Christ, partly to nurture his or her own faith, and partly to aid him or her in service to God and people. This is why the disciple sees his or her regular participation in the Eucharist and other liturgical celebrations of the faith of the church as vital to his or her spiritual growth and development (Matt. 18:20; Mark 14:22-25; Luke 22:15-20; 1 Cor. 11:23-25).

A disciple is one who is submitted to God's appointed authorities over his life and ministry (1 Peter 5:5,6; Heb. 13:17).

A disciple is one who has a learner's attitude. He or she is a humble person, a teachable person. The disciple is hungry for divine wisdom (Rom. 12:3, 16; Prov. 10:17; 12:1; 27:7).

A disciple is one who is actively involved in bringing the people he or she meets to an encounter with Jesus Christ. The disciple is involved in God's mission in this world (Matt. 6:33; 28:19-20; Acts 1:8; John 4:35).

Table 7-2 Profile of a Disciple

I believe that the edification process involves four major stages: 1) the telling stage, 2) the showing stage, 3) the doing stage, and 4) the accountability stage. My goal is to establish basic biblical beliefs and practices in the life of the convert so that he or she has a solid spiritual foundation upon which to build. The profile of a disciple described in Table 7-2 describes what I would like to see produced in the lives of these individuals.

A Call to Rethink the Church

Many contemporary theologians and authors are calling for a new understanding or paradigm of the church (Snyder 1975, Banks 1994, Mead 1991, Ogden 1990). Hendrik Kraemer understands that the first and foremost qualification of the church is that it is a "community which belongs to Christ and is in Christ" (1958:100). In this sense Kraemer uses the concept of "church" interchangeably with "people of God."

This emphasis on the church as a close-knit community of faith which meets in small home-groups is central to my approach to the ministry in France. The goal of my ministry in France is not to develop a denomination, sect, or association, but a spiritual community. [3]

This goal is by no means unique to my ministry. There are many other groups working in France to establish the church, the fellowship of the Body of Christ. There are, however, divergent opinions as to the structure that this "people" or "spiritual family" should have and the most appropriate means for giving birth to this faith community.

Most of the North American evangelical missionaries ministering in France in recent times have had the goal of establishing congregations of believers. This goal is understandable when one considers the importance the Scriptures place on the believing communities. In order to "plant" one of these congregations the missionaries typically use methods such as open-air meetings, literature distribution, the projection of gospel films, door-to-door visitation, telephone surveys and media advertisement in order to draw the French to meetings where the verbal communication of the gospel message is presented. On occasion these meetings take place in a building which has a sign hanging over the door indicating the Protestant or evangelical identity of the group. As I have already pointed out, such methods meet with only limited success.

Even when the evangelistic methods employed are less formal (such as a small Bible study group in a home, or an informal conversation over dinner), the goal of the missionary is often to incorporate the individual into his or her evangelical group. This would mean, of course, that the individual would be in effect converting from Catholicism to Protestantism. We have already noted that this approach creates a formidable barrier in the heart and mind of the average Frenchman which is almost impossible to overcome.

A worker is one who evidences growth in the virtues and skills listed under my profile of a disciple (1 Tim. 4:15-16).

A worker is one who has demonstrated his or her ability to lead people to Christ (Matt. 4:19).

A worker is one who has raised up at least one new follower of Christ who meets the qualifications of our profile of a disciple. He or she is currently engaged in the spiritual accompanying of young believers (2 Tim. 2:2).

A worker is one who has made a public commitment to work with, encourage, support, and pray for other disciples who share his or her purpose in life. The worker pools his or her abilities and resources with other workers with the intent of evangelizing the lost and establishing the believers (Ecc. 4:9-10; Col. 2:6-7).

Table 7-3 Profile of a Worker

In the actual historical and cultural context of post-Christendom France we have not found it necessary to call our converts to sever their ties with the Catholic Church. First, because we have recognized the presence of truly converted, obedient followers of Jesus Christ within the ranks of the Catholic Church. Second, because the Catholic Church has not shown hostility toward our converts who have come back to their church through our ministry. Third, because in several instances these converts from our ministry have been able to influence by their lives and witness the life of their parish, and bring encouragement to their parish priest. For example, several of our "disciples" are involved teaching catechism in their respective parishes. The message that they are sharing is biblical, evangelical, and Roman Catholic. In fact, we have found that these French disciples of Christ have become "sought after" by the Catholic community because of their biblical competence, their quality of life, their solid convictions, and their clear and effective witness. A last reason why we do not feel it necessary to call our converts to sever all ties with the French Catholic Church is that the sacraments and liturgical gatherings of the Catholic Church are a necessary source of spiritual strengthening and encouragement for these believers.

The disciples of Christ for whom we have an "equipping" role have learned to feed their spiritual hunger through daily time spent with Christ. They are also involved in small group Bible studies where they are taught, stimulated and encouraged in their faith. They are tied into the larger faith community and nurtured through regular Eucharistic celebrations and the other sacraments of the Catholic Church. They are learning through the Scriptures and in relationship to their own Christian tradition whether or not we, or anyone else, is teaching them false doctrine (Acts 17:11). They are growing in their openness and accountability to the other members of their Bible study group, and they are learning to assume responsibility for the spiritual well-being of the others.

One of my goals as an evangelical Protestant missionary is to equip these individuals so as to make them fruitful in their witness for Christ (Eph. 4:11-12). To do this I continue to deepen their understanding of the basics of the Christian life, particularly in the areas of humility, commitment to others, spiritual reproduction and multiplication, and service to others. Our role is to keep these disciples in an environment where growth can occur.

What About Participation at Mass?

Many of my evangelical Protestant friends and colleagues are concerned that by allowing those I accompany in the faith to participate at Mass, I am in some way condoning the "erroneous doctrines of the Catholic Church." This seems to be a North American fundamentalist concept which is often used as the basis for separation from believers with whom one disagrees. In the next chapter I will share how I handle those areas where Protestants and Roman Catholics have been unable to come to common understandings and agreement. At this point I will state simply that I don't condone all of the teachings, doctrines and practices of the Roman Catholic Church any more than I wholeheartedly endorse all of the doctrines, practices or teachings of the Missionary Church (of which I am an ordained minister).

In reality, I do more than *allow* those I accompany in the faith to attend Mass—I actively *model* and *promote* that participation. The overwhelming majority of people to whom I have ministered in Christ's name were non-practicing Catholic atheists when we met. Most of these individuals did not recognize their need for the liturgy or sacraments of the Catholic Church. As a consequence, I have found myself obliged to adopt an active and aggressive advocacy on behalf of the Catholic Church (through both my own example and teaching). Had I taken a neutral stance the majority of those to whom I have ministered would either be the sort of believer who wanders from one small evangelical Protestant group to the next, or they would have attempted to live their faith in independent isolation from the larger faith community. Both of those options have proven counter-productive.

Training Lay Leaders

Another of my objectives is to train leaders for service to the believing communities which result from my ministry as an evangelical Protestant missionary. My desire is that leaders be trained and empowered to care for and "coach" the "disciples" and "workers" as together they minister to their world in Jesus' name. Elton Trueblood describes this kind of leadership:

> Some are coming to believe that the least inadequate or distorting term for a spiritual leader in a congregation is "coach." ... The glory of the coach is that of being the discoverer, the developer, and the trainer of the powers of other men (and women). But this is exactly what we mean when we use the Biblical terminology about the equipping ministry ... Since the equipping minister must not be above the heat of the battle, he (or she) is, ideally, not only a coach, but a "playing coach," sometimes carrying the ball himself (or herself) and sometimes seeing to it that another carries it. Thus, he (or she) is both a minister and the encourager, a teacher and a developer of his (or her) fellow ministers, who are the members of the Church of Christ. The mark of his (or her) success is not the amount of attention which he (or she) can focus upon himself (or herself), but the redemptive character which emerges in the entire congregation or team. Fundamentally, he (or she) is called to be a catalytic agent, often making a radical difference while being relatively inconspicuous. (1967:43-44)

Again I turn to the example of Jesus Christ to find the model upon which I base my strategy for the development of leaders. In Mark 3:14 we read: "He appointed twelve—designating them apostles—that they might be with him and that he might send them out to preach and to have authority to drive out demons." We find in this text from Scripture the principle of in-depth personal training involving large amounts of time spent together in a variety of situations.

A leader is one who evidences growth in the virtues and skills listed under my profile of a worker (1 Tim. 3:1-7).

A leader is one who has a volunteer spirit. He or she quickly discerns needs and takes action to find solutions to those needs (Isaiah 6:8).

A leader is one who has become a pacesetter to the rest of the believing community (Phil. 4:9).

A leader is one who has become a reproducer of converts who are becoming disciples and disciples who are becoming workers (2 Tim. 2:2).

A leader is one who has learned how to study the Word of God and how to pass on to others what God is teaching him or her. He/she has become an excellent Bible study leader (Luke 24:32, 45).

A leader is one who has developed sensitivity to God's leading in his or her life (Acts 24:16).

A leader is one who has learned to think. He or she knows how to encourage and rebuke with all authority (Titus 2:15).

A leader is one who has a heart for others. He or she sees people as "precious in God's sight" (Josh. 4:24).

A leader is a person who has his or her priorities established by the Word of God (John 14:21). He or she is a person who has learned to say "no" to the many distractions that cross an individual's life. He or she has resolved to stay with whatever task God has given until he or she sees it accomplished.

Table 7-4 Profile of a Leader

Hesselgrave has observed that it is not enough that certain believers display the potential for leadership. As they give evidence of spiritual growth, they must be given the appropriate opportunities to utilize their potential and develop as leader/coaches (1982:359). This process is demanding for both the missionary and the emerging leader, but the results justify the sacrifices involved.

I believe that the training for leadership deals with developing Scriptural convictions and ministry skills in such areas as family life, personal counseling, world vision, spiritual warfare, priorities and balance, goal setting, time management, spiritual gifts, forming and leading small groups, discernment and perspective, and servant-leadership.

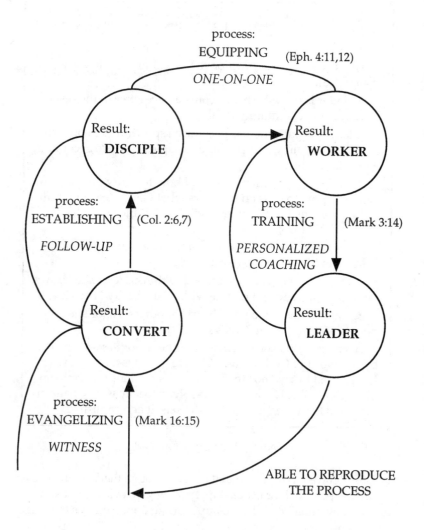

Figure 2

Descriptive Chart of Ministry in France

I find it important to note that since these individuals (converted to faith in Jesus Christ and brought to spiritual maturity within the context of the local faith communities to which we have given birth and through the liturgy and sacraments of the Catholic Church) are fully integrated into their local parish, their capacity for spiritual leadership should be acknowledged both by the members of our "faith community" and by the hierarchy of the French Catholic Church. Together with the local priests and bishop we discern the places of leadership which they can occupy and the ministries they can perform, considering their unique distinctives as a product of our evangelical Protestant missionary endeavor.

These leaders face some unusual problems. They have the delicate task of leading the "converts," "disciples," and "workers" in discerning and sorting out those forms of religious practice which they can (and must) continue in order to remain true to the Scriptures and to the faith tradition which they have received from their French Catholic heritage. They must also encourage the members of the faith community to hold firm, to obediently follow Christ in what is often a hostile secularized environment.

Concluding Thoughts

The French believers, fruit of my ministry, are placed in a unique position. They have learned to believe in the foundational truths of Scripture, many of which are the doctrinal heritage of the Reformation, yet they continue to live and practice their faith in an environment which is often hostile to evangelicalism. Their faith is biblical, and as such is often questioned by the people with whom they live. Sometimes they are accused of becoming Protestants, or Fundamentalists, and at times they are told that they are not really Catholic at all. On occasion they have strong prejudices against their own Roman Catholic Church (although they would never abandon it), which hamper their worship experience. And it must be stated that there are some parish situations where they find it impossible to worship at all because of their new-found convictions.

We have also noted that the French culture, as such, is opposed to what these believers hold to be true.

It is in such an environment, then, that we must turn over responsibility for the ministry to the French themselves. In one sense, the strategy and approach to ministry that I describe in these chapters facilitate the transition from evangelical Protestant missionary to

French Catholic national. My ministry has no official organizational structure, no physical point of identity. I have no church buildings, no schools. The only thing that I have to turn over to the French is the ministry itself.

Not only is the question of what is turned over to the French simplified by this approach to the ministry, but so is the question of when to turn the ministry over to them. Someone has said that in most cases it is almost as important that pioneers know when and how to leave a new work, as that they know when and where to undertake it in the first place. How do we know when those we have accompanied in the faith are able to stand on their own? When the ministry that they represent is functioning in each of the areas which we have discussed in this chapter: pagans are becoming converts, converts are becoming disciples, disciples are being banded together and are becoming active workers, and leaders are emerging from their ranks to assume responsibility for their spiritual well-being (see Figure 2).

We realize that our ministry will suffer greatly if the withdrawal of the missionaries comes either too soon or too late. As Hesselgrave puts it: "The baton must be passed to the next runner. When the pioneer leaves the race without passing on the baton, he departs too soon. When he continues to hold the baton until he has exhausted his time and resources, it may be too late" (1980:394). The approach to ministry that we have adopted makes our "passing on of the baton" a gradual process. We work ourselves out of a job as the French grow into ministry.

We have watched this happen as new ministries have sprung up around France through the initiative of several of the disciples from our original outreach in Normandy. In certain places the local Catholic bishops have taken an active part in these initiatives. Thus, to a certain extent the ministry that we began back in 1979 has already gone full-circle.

Notes

1. (p. 84) In a fascinating article entitled "Proselytism, Mission, and the Bible," Eugene P. Heideman indicates that in both the Old and the New Testaments conversion was not a call to a change of community so much as it was a call to new obedience to God. To illustrate this point from the New Testament Heideman points to the Day of Pentecost when Peter called upon the crowd of Jews and proselytes "from every

nation" to repent and be baptized, without expecting them to change their community identity. Even the rite of baptism did not, according to Heideman, entail a change from one human community to another:

> Conversion and baptism did not mean a change in human community or citizenship in the New Testament. As we have already noted, throughout the New Testament, Jews who are baptized remain Jews and continue to identify with the temple and the synagogue. The Samaritans, the Ethiopian eunuch, and Cornelius the Roman do not change citizenship when they become followers of Jesus. Rather than a change of affiliation in the human community of converts, the undergirding idea of being 'in Christ' is to experience a new birth 'from above' (John 3:3) and to gain citizenship in heaven (Phil. 3:20).
>
> Baptism today is often viewed both within the church and by those outside as the rite that symbolized the breach in relationships whereby a person leaves one community to become a member of another. Baptism in the New Testament, however, did not have that character. (1996:11)

2. (p. 85) Hesselgrave refers to the work of Edward Hall on learning:

> A most helpful distinction has been made by the anthropologist Edward T. Hall. He believes that learning takes place at three levels: the formal level (mistake-correction); the informal level (imitation of models); and the technical level (from a teacher). One of Hall's major contentions is that a far greater proportion of learning than we may suppose takes place at the informal level. One of the implications of this is that much more attention needs to be given to the modeling of biblical truth. Unless truth is exemplified and modeled in terms of changed behavior, its mere recitation probably is not nearly as effective as we ordinarily suppose. This is especially the case in the pioneer situation. (1982:309)

3. (p. 89) A Christian community is comprised of all of the saints of God in a given locality who, in love, take careful note of each other's spiritual, social, mental, and physical welfare and development (Heb. 10:24-25). When I speak of a "community," I am making reference to what the Reformers called the *coetus fidelium* (the communion of believers, who are united in the bond of the Spirit), while they referred to the institutional church as the *mater fidelium* (the mother of the believers).

The Reformation brought the truth to the foreground once more that the essence of the church is not found in the external organization of the church, but in the church as the *communio sanctorum*. For both Luther and Calvin the church was first and foremost the community of the saints—that is, the community of those who believe and are sanctified in Christ, and who are joined to Him as their Head.

The use of the word *koinonia* underlines this concept of the church as the communion or fellowship of God's people, called out of the world and separated to live for Him. Most frequently the New Testament word *ekklesia* designates a circle of believers in some definite locality, a local church, irrespective of the question whether these believers are or are not assembled for worship. While some passages contain the idea that they are assembled (Acts 5:11; 11:26; 1 Cor. 11:18; 14:19, 28, 35), others do not (Rom. 16:4; 1 Cor. 16:1; Gal. 1:2; 1 Thess. 2:14). Both words, *koinonia* and *ekklesia*, speak to the communion of those who have been spiritually united with Christ.

Chapter 8

And When We Don't Agree

There is a very important consideration which we must address as evangelical Protestant missionaries working in French Catholic culture. It is the question of how the followers of Christ can live together in the unity of the Spirit, keeping the bond of peace even when they don't agree. In his address to the Chicago Consultation on Partnership in Mission in Western Europe, Arthur Glasser maintained that one of the major concerns of Jesus Christ for His church is for its unity:

> What are the concerns of Jesus Christ for his church? He prayed for its unity; that is the first thing. He prayed more for its unity than anything else because no one segment of the church has all the truth. Every segment of the church is weak and wobbly, every segment could fade into the wallpaper and disappear.
>
> So He said they must come together, they must listen to one another, they must express somehow their oneness, be one!
>
> The New Testament places much more stress on the unity of the church than it does on the whole possession of the truth because, unless people are willing to face one another, listen to one another, they will never come to an understanding of the truth. As you have in Ephesians 4, the first few verses, it is through expressing unity that you come to the unity of the faith and the knowledge of the Son of God. Nobody has all the answers. (Bayssat 1986:10)

Evangelicals assert that the unity of the Church is not primarily of an external, but of an internal and spiritual character. It is the unity of the mystical body of Jesus Christ, of which all believers are members. This body is controlled by one Head, Jesus Christ, who is also the King of the church, and is animated by one Spirit, the Spirit of Christ.

This unity implies that all those who belong to the church share in the same faith, are cemented together by the common bond of love, and have the same glorious outlook upon the future (Eph. 4:4-6).

1 Corinthians 12:13 tells how a person enters the mystical body of Jesus Christ: "For we were all baptized by one Spirit into one Body—whether Jews or Greeks, slave or free—and we were all given one Spirit to drink." In verses 12 and 13 the Apostle Paul refers to "one Body" four times to emphasize body unity. [1] In God's eyes the followers of Christ are one, and salvation is the initial point of their unity. John MacArthur Jr. points this out so clearly in his book, *The Church, the Body of Christ*:

> Every biblical metaphor of the Church, without exception, empha-sizes its unity. The Church is one Bride with one Husband; one Flock with one Shepherd; one set of branches on one Vine; one Kingdom with one King; one Family with one Father; one Building with one Foundation; one Body with one Head, Jesus Christ. (1973:19)

That Jesus taught that His followers were to be undivided in John 13:34-35 and John 17:20-23 is above debate. This was also the teaching of the first century Christian leaders, as Kenneth Scott Latourette has observed:

> The ideal of the Church appears again and again in the early Christian documents which compose the New Testament and which reflect the convictions of leaders in the primitive Christian fellowship. To these leaders the Church was to be inclusive and one. They shared the purpose of Jesus which was transmitted through "the Gospel according to John" that all believers in Him should be as united as were He and the Father. (1975:113)

The desire for unity and the possibility of its realization are not, then, necessarily wrong. In fact, the fear of unity is a fairly recent development in traditional Protestantism. Harold Rowdon has shown that the Edinburgh Conference of 1910 was really fathered by evan-gelical Protestants (1967:49-71). All through the nineteenth century, the cause of Christian unity was almost completely the cause of the evangelicals. Only subsequently did others become interested in it. And some time after 1910, because of the interest of those from other theological persuasions, the ecumenical movement was abandoned by the evangelicals (Wells 1973:107).

In the next chapter I will attempt to describe the kind of unity which I think we must experience with our brothers and sisters in Christ who belong to different Christian faith traditions than our own. Whatever ecumenical stance I might have developed through the years is the result of continually searching for the means by which we can reach out in the name of Christ to individuals who identify themselves with the Catholic subsociety of French culture. My desire has been to remain faithful to the gospel and to my own Christian heritage, which is a product of the Reformation. At the same time I realize that I must be careful not to allow strife, haggling over theological positions, and dissension to obstruct the ministry to which God has called me in His world. I believe that we must work diligently to keep the avenues of service open to the work of the Holy Spirit so that He can accomplish His purposes in the lives of the French who are attentive to our witness.

God has called me to minister in a country where millions of people are strangers to the gospel, and other millions, nominally Christians, are in need of evangelizing. I cannot compromise the essentials of the gospel; neither can I afford to harbor tensions, prejudices and divisions which would stand as obstacles in the path of my evangelistic, God-given mission.

As we look at the question of our disagreements, one of the first issues that we must address is: Are the divisions between the evangelical Protestants and the Roman Catholics of past generations still valid? Or, have the Roman Catholics and Protestant evangelicals grown and changed through the centuries and come to new levels of common understanding and agreement? In other words, do we accurately appraise the nature of our present disagreements?

Is the Catholic Church Changing?

John Stott has written concerning the Catholic Church:

> For over 400 years Protestants and Roman Catholics have remained in the entrenched positions into which they dug themselves at the Reformation. Just about their only contact has been to lob theological grenades at one another across a deserted no-man's land. The argument was largely restricted to the terms of the Reformation Confessions and the Decrees of the Council of Trent. The polemics on both sides have been rigid and harsh.
>
> *These days are over. For Rome has changed and is continuing to change, despite her claim to changelessness.* (quoted in Wells 1973:i; *emphasis mine*)

David Wells explains the reasons why both the Roman Catholics and the Protestant evangelicals have maintained that the Catholic Church does not change:

Catholic apologists in the seventeenth and eighteenth centuries claimed that Rome never changes, and Protestants, for their own reasons, believed them. It was a myth nourished by mutual consent. For Roman Catholics, it was the only defensive posture they felt they could take against the Protestant charge that they had perverted the gospel. How could this be, they retorted, when seventeenth-century Rome believed precisely to the letter what the first-century apostles had believed? The Roman Catholic Church had neither added nor subtracted one iota to or from the biblical teaching. In short, Rome never changes.

Protestants accepted the Catholic claim to support their own contention that Roman theology had always been uniformly bad. It had never changed for the better, but only, perhaps, for the worse. Protestant apologists were quite certain that Rome had perverted the biblical teaching early in her history. Indeed, they said, this defection was so well established in the official pronouncements of the Church that a return to true biblical teaching was impossible. The Reformation had demonstrated this fact. Rome never changes. (Wells 1976:7)

While some evangelicals continue to insist that the Catholic Church will never change, others are actively working with and within the Church. The words of the World Evangelical Fellowship reflect on the confusion of the present situation:

During the past centuries, and especially in recent decades, significant changes are evident along many fronts. There is great ferment in Roman Catholic circles and the picture is far from clear. In it all we welcome every hopeful sign pointing to the revival of true apostolic faith. We experience continuing dismay, however, whenever the gospel is blurred or eclipsed. It seems sometimes that everything is changing, when at times nothing has changed. (World Evangelical Fellowship 1986:9)

David Wells points out that the changes in the Catholic Church have made it possible for dialogue between evangelical Protestants and some Catholics:

Evangelical Protestants have discovered that there are Catholics who are nearer to their own position than are those Protestants who have been influenced by, say, the new secular and political theologies. By the same token, a Catholic with evangelical concerns may find more kinship with conservative Protestants than he does with "progressive" friends in his own church. Ideological differences are more important than denominational distinctives. Hitherto, the differences between evangelical Protestants and Catholics were at one and the same time ideological and denominational; in some instances they may now be denominational alone. (1976:136)

In his address to the International Congress on World Evangelism which was held in Lausanne, Switzerland, Mr. Atallah, the Quebec Director of InterVarsity Christian Fellowship, described the recent changes within the Roman Catholic Church and analyzed them briefly. According to Atallah these trends are:

> The reinterpretation of dogma.
> A new emphasis on Scripture.
> The awakening of religious experience.
> The decentralization of authority.

The following are some of the conclusions he drew from the examination of these trends:

> The new interest in the Scriptures among Catholics has made them open to those who are willing to expound the Word to them ... as well as participating with Roman Catholics in small Bible study groups, evangelical Protestants need to be willing to spend time with believing Catholics. Fellowship should be based upon mutual life in Christ rather than on doctrinal agreement. (1975:884)

In his article entitled, "Contemporary Dialogues with Traditional Catholicism," Harold O. J. Brown shares his conviction that the changes within the Catholic Church have made it possible for increasing numbers of Catholics to do within their church what only two decades ago they found hard to achieve without leaving it: come to a simple, straightforward gospel faith in the free salvation earned once for all in the finished work of Jesus Christ, and to the attitudes of trust and assurance and the practices of piety that are appropriate to that faith (1976:148). He continues by affirming that:

> Formerly such awakening and conversion seemed automatically to require the Catholic to leave his old church and join an evangelical fellowship. This was clearly evangelization. Indeed, in past decades it was not at all unusual for a Catholic who began to entertain an evangelical understanding of the Christian faith to be forced out of the Roman church. Today, very little such pressure is put on evangelically awakened Catholics by their church. If the Roman Catholic Church is not in a position to discipline priests, or even professors of theology who appear to be theological liberals and moral relativists and to reject some of the fundamental truths and most basic moral obligations of Christian faith, it is not apt to take steps against those who are merely evangelically inclined. (1976:151)

In our day, a paradoxical situation has arisen: Catholic interest in the Bible has grown to an unprecedented extent, but the result is not what evangelical Protestants expected. It has not produced widespread defection among Catholics or mass conversion to Protestantism in any form. Thus the time-honored Protestant conviction that the way to win (proselytize) Roman Catholics is to "get them into the Bible" is not proving true. At least it is not working out that way. Catholics are regularly urged by their church to read the Bible and adopt other formal and informal devotional practices previously typical of Protestantism; they join Bible studies and prayer groups, but not Protestant churches. [2]

In his editorial entitled, "Church on the Move (For the evangelical, the most exciting change in Roman Catholicism is the new freedom for the gospel)," Kenneth Kantzer writes a summary of how he feels evangelicals should be affected by these changes within Roman Catholicism:

> How does all this affect the evangelical? First, we should continue to dialogue. To refuse to dialogue would be to say two things no evangelical wants to say: (1) We are not interested in our Lord's desire to have a united church, and (2) We evangelicals have nothing to learn from anyone. Dialogue need not be compromise. It can be an effective means of evangelism, and it can be a great source of humble learning on the part of those who are willing to listen.
>
> Second, we can rejoice with the new-found evangelicals in the Roman Catholic church. We can encourage them. We can learn from them. We need not attack what we deem to be holdovers from Roman Catholic doctrine, but we can exalt the Lord with them and urge them to join us in testing faith by the Holy Scripture.
>
> Third, we should take advantage of the freedom newly allowed in the Roman church. We should encourage this freedom in the direction of a saving faith in Jesus Christ and in the authority of Scripture. We should remind those who are sitting uneasily on traditional Roman Catholic doctrine and are attracted by rampant liberalism that true freedom is not freedom from all authority or freedom from truth. Rather, it provides for a voluntary acceptance of truth and leads us to obey the holy and all-wise God of the universe. (1986:17)

Catholic Evangelicals?

The people that we have just quoted all recognize a stream of evangelicalism that runs deep in the Roman Catholic church. [3] The

Catholic evangelicals are concerned to maintain continuity with the tradition of the whole church. Yet, there is within this spiritual current a stress on evangelical essentials within the context of Catholic faith. These believers make a serious attempt to uphold the inspiration and infallibility of Scripture but without getting bogged down in interminable warfare over inerrancy. And, not content with spiritual unity, they press on to the ideal of the visible unity of the church.

Donald Bloesch, one of the foremost theologians in the evangelical world today, has observed that:

> Catholic evangelicals not only draw on the Reformation and the post-Reformation purification movements of Pietism and Puritanism, but they also encourage a renewed appreciation for pre-Reformation evangelicalism. In striving for a revitalized church in our time, they seek to enlist the support not only of the Reformers but also of the church fathers and doctors of the medieval church. Whereas fundamentalists and many Pentecostals look to separatist, nonconformist groups like the Donatists, the Montanists, the Novatians and the Waldensians, catholic evangelicals appeal to the mainstream of the church, particularly to the early fathers. (1983:49)

The French Catholic evangelicals with whom I have been in dialogue are quickly disturbed by the activism that pervades much of North American Protestant evangelicalism. They find the evangelical Protestant missionary's fascination with communication skills over sound theology and church growth techniques over sound ecclesiology as a sign of North American evangelical capitulation to the technological materialism of our age. These men and women of God are acutely aware of the need for training in discipleship. They emphasize evangelism and nurture: "In line with the catholic tradition at its best, catholic evangelicals stress being before doing, faith before works, contemplation before action" (Bloesch 1983:49). For these believers, growth in faith is almost as important as the decision of faith.

Bloesch points out that these followers of Jesus continually seek to distinguish a vital relationship with Christ from formalistic orthodoxy or ecclesiasticism:

> Even though it (catholic evangelicalism) makes an important place for sacraments and an ordained ministry, it eschews sacramentalism and sacerdotalism. Like the Puritans, it also objects to unnecessary or over elaborate symbolism in the church and to a concern for vestments and liturgy over inward faith and experience. Nonetheless, with Calvin and other mainline Reformers, it also regards with disapproval an unstructured or totally free service of worship.

It favors a liturgy of the Word and the sacrament, but with the sacrament subordinated to the Word. Its objections to Roman Catholicism arise, at least partly, out of the conviction that catholicity is unnecessarily confined to one particular tradition in the church; therefore, the Church of Rome is not catholic enough. (1983:51)

The new stirrings of evangelical sentiment within French Roman Catholicism are a sign that all is not lost and that many missionaries are urging their converts to leave the Catholic Church prematurely and for the wrong reasons. The presence of this evangelical current in French Roman Catholicism means that those whom we accompany in the faith can find many areas of shared belief and practice within the Catholic fold. While there is much diversity among the followers of Christ, I believe that evangelicals of all varieties have much more in common with each other than with liberalism or modernism.

We See Through a Glass Darkly

In 1 Corinthians 13:12 the Apostle Paul writes that: "At present we are men looking at puzzling reflections in a mirror. The time will come when we shall see reality whole and face to face! At present all I know is a fraction of the truth, but the time will come when I shall know it as fully as God knows me" (Phillips).

Why is it that we have such a difficult time admitting that we can't see all of God's truth? Why are we so much slower than the Apostle Paul to acknowledge that today we only know in part?

I think that these words of the Apostle remind us of a very important element of human experience with which we must come to grips. Paul's words underline the truth of our own ethnocentricity. We see part of the truth and assume that we have seen it all. We get so accustomed to looking at reality through our own dirty window that after a while we no longer notice how the dirt obstructs our view.

I am constantly reminded of this when I meet North Americans who have never lived outside of the United States. They tend to think that the American way of understanding and living life is the best. More often than not, these North Americans are convinced that their customs, beliefs and practices are superior to those of the other peoples of the world. They swear that they live as they do because the "American way" is the best way. They resist the notion that they do things the way they do because that is how they have learned to live.

They naively think that they are totally objective and that if they ever discover a system of government or type of civilization that is better than theirs, then they would adopt it as their own.

Live for any length of time in other cultures and you will discover that the members of those societies also feel that their way of life is the most complete and responds the most appropriately to the realities of human existence.

The irony is that we all know that there is no perfect human society. The American way of life has its flaws and weaknesses. The French way of doing things is not the best.

While we will sometimes admit to our cultural ethnocentricity, we find it more difficult to acknowledge that we are ecclesiologically and theologically ethnocentric. Many of us will go to the grave swearing that we have understood God's revealed truth in all of its fullness. Such a self-assured prideful attitude is the source of many of the divisions in the church today.

Of all the people who could claim to see all the truth, one would think that the Apostle Paul would have that confidence. Yet his words are: "Now we see things imperfectly, as in a poor mirror, but then we will see everything with perfect clarity. *All that I know is partial and incomplete*, but then I will know everything completely, just as God knows me" (1 Cor. 13:12, New Living Translation, *emphasis added*). Before we make a major issue of our points of disagreement with the followers of Jesus who don't see things exactly as we do, perhaps we need to acknowledge our own inability to appropriate the truth.

Figure 3 illustrates the limitations that both the evangelical Protestants and the Roman Catholics experience as they view God's truth only partially and incompletely. I contend that as they look at God's truth revealed in the person of Jesus, the Scriptures, and the experience of the people of God, they do see many of the same truths. They also have a vision of some of God's truth that is hidden from the direct view of the other. It is in these areas that there is often disagreement and conflict. It is also in these areas that there is room to help the other faith community expand its vision.

You will also notice from Figure 3 that the perspective of both faith communities extends beyond the limits of God's truth. By drawing the figure in this way I hope to illustrate the fact that wherever people are involved in God's plan there is a mixture of the human with the divine. In other words, there are practices and beliefs held by the followers of Christ, regardless of their origin or culture, that are not a part of God's revealed truth. In the light of such practices, what are we to do?

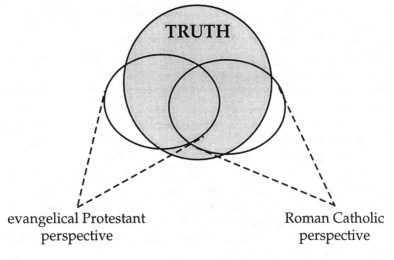

Figure 3:

True But Partial Vision of God's Truth

Prophet or Herald?

What is the role of a missionary? I would argue that with rare exceptions, a missionary is to be a herald rather than a prophet!

I use the term "herald" to speak of the individual who announces something or someone. Paul speaks of this missional activity when he writes:

> How can they call on the one they have not believed in? And how can they believe in the one of whom they have not heard? And how can they hear without someone preaching to them? And how can they preach unless they are sent? As it is written, 'How beautiful are the feet of those who bring good news!' (Rom. 10:14-15).

I propose that the herald's message is primarily received by the receptors as good news!

The prophet, on the other hand, denounces sin and proclaims judgment. The prophet is typically not a carrier of "good news." I know some evangelical Protestant missionaries who feel that it is their role to be prophets to the French Catholic population. These individuals spend their time and energy decrying the "heresies" and falsehoods they see in the Catholic faith.

I believe that the missionary is rarely, if ever, called by God to be a prophet! At least not to the people to whom he or she has been sent (one notable Scriptural exception to this principle is Jonah). I believe that the prophetic voice must be that of a cultural "insider" and the missionary will never reach that status. No matter how well integrated and adapted to the host culture, no matter how linguistically gifted the individual missionary might be, he or she will never be able to fully enter into the worldview of the receptor society. To one degree or another, the missionary will always possess an "etic" rather than "emic" perspective.

I take the position that the missionary should almost never be the prophetic voice for a number of other reasons. First, because people respond poorly to an outsider who attempts to play the role of a prophet. I hear the French complain about different elements of their culture all the time. But, do you know what happens if I ever agree with them? Then they change their position and defend the same things that they were just criticizing. I dare not even smile in agreement or nod my head when I hear them criticize their country or their church. And Americans are the same way. We are allowed to criticize ourselves, but an outsider had better not join in.

A second reason why I feel that only a cultural insider can be the prophet is because the cultural insider, unlike missionaries, knows that he or she cannot leave the country if things go bad. Missionaries are not obliged to live "forever" in the community or area where they are ministering and so they don't typically take a long-term approach. North American evangelical Protestant missionaries are anxious to go into an area, do their thing, and get out. The people to whom they are ministering have a different view of the situation. The members of the receptor society have years of experience in the situations which the missionaries are just entering, and they will probably be in those same relationships and situations after the missionaries have left the scene. When missionaries lead their converts to judge, condemn and denounce religious beliefs and practices that they find offensive, the young believers will have to live with those damaged relationships for the rest of their lives.

For these reasons I believe that the evangelical Protestant missionary serving in post-Christendom lands is not called by God to denounce anyone or anything. Instead I am convinced that we are commissioned by God to announce Christ. Instead of complaining about how dark we perceive it to be, we should turn on the light. In our own case this means that instead of focusing on what we perceive to be wrong with Catholicism, we should focus on our common faith in Christ and on our common task of leading men and women, boys and girls, to embrace the Savior.

> Have nothing to do with stupid, senseless controversies; you know that they breed quarrels. (2 Tim. 2:23 RSV)

> He will also judge those who cause divisions. Void of the love of God, they look to their own advantage and not to the unity of the church: for small and trifling reasons they rend the great and glorious body of Christ into pieces. (Irenaeus)

The areas where we don't agree with the Catholic Church should not be our focus! Jesus promised His followers that the Holy Spirit would give them direction and teach them all He Himself had said (John 14:26). A little later Jesus said that the Spirit would guide His followers into truth and bring glory to the Son (John 16:13-15). It is the Spirit, not the missionary, who has been sent to convict of sin, righteousness and judgment (John 16:8). Do we really believe these words of Christ? Or do we feel as if we need to help the Holy Spirit of the Living God to accomplish His task?

North American Protestant evangelical missionaries have a present opportunity for aggressive evangelism that may not come again. By the next generation the theological confusion and liberal thought of many of the Catholic clergy may well spoil the present hunger of masses of French Catholics. We must learn how to take advantage of the unique historical and cultural situation in which we have been called to announce Christ. As the World Evangelical Fellowship put it: "We are constrained by the commission of our Lord (2 Cor. 5:18-20) and by the love of Christ (2 Cor. 5:14) to proclaim the gospel to all people, including those who are Roman Catholic" (1986:44).

The Path of Least Resistance

No matter the path we choose in announcing Christ in a country like France, there will be resistance. First there is the resistance that comes from the god of this age who "has blinded the minds of unbelievers, so that they cannot see the light of the gospel of the glory of Christ" (2 Cor. 4:2). This resistance must be overcome by fervent prayer, for God alone can make His light shine in human hearts (2 Cor. 4:6).

A second kind of resistance which we encounter as we proclaim the person and teaching of the Lord Jesus Christ in modern France is what the Apostle Paul referred to as the "foolishness" of the cross (1 Cor. 1:18). The average Frenchman cannot conceptualize how the death and resurrection of Jesus of Nazareth some two thousand years ago could possibly have any relevance for his life today. Most of the French people that I know feel that the message and teachings of Christ were perhaps helpful back when He lived, but that they are outdated and irrelevant today. Others, blinded by their own pride, refuse to acknowledge their need of a Savior. Many find the moral and ethical instructions of our Lord impractical and unlivable in the modern world. This constitutes a very real and persistent resistance to our witness.

What our approach to the missionary task in post-Christendom France does, however, is eliminate the resistance of social stigma attached to those who change their Catholic identity and become members of an evangelical Protestant "sect." By emphasizing what we have in common with our Catholic brothers and sisters in Christ, and by teaching our converts how to ratify the baptism they received as children, we allow whatever resistance they receive from others to be because of their positive witness for Christ.

The testimony of one couple whom we led to the Savior some years ago illustrates this point. These university students had been living together for two years before we met. When they both knelt in our living room, confessed their sinful ways, and asked Jesus Christ to become the Lord and Master of their lives, we had never addressed the issue of their sexual relationship. However, in the days that followed their conversion they decided (unknown to me) that as followers of Christ they could no longer continue to have sexual relations until their relationship was established in the sacrament of marriage.

This decision was put to the test a short time later, when this couple returned to the family farm during a school break. On that occasion the young man in question told his father that he and his girlfriend would not be using the same bedroom as had been their custom in the past.

The father asked: "Are you experiencing difficulties in your relationship? Do you still love each other?"

To which this young convert replied: "Dad, we love each other today more than ever before!"

"Then what is the matter?" asked the father.

"We have made a new commitment of our lives to Jesus Christ and we do not think that He would want us to continue having sexual relations until after we are married," replied my friend.

Do you know what this conservative French Catholic farmer's response was to this situation? First, he tried to persuade his son to go see a psychiatrist for professional help. Second, he invited me to come to the village, where for almost eight hours non-stop, I was interviewed by family members and the local priest in an attempt to discern if this young couple had not been seduced by some sort of sect. At the end of that day together, as I was boarding the train for the three-hour trip home, the father said to me: "Dave, I want to believe that you are a true follower of Christ and not a member of a sect; I hope that I will not be disappointed."

This story illustrates that when French men and women embrace Christ and begin to take his teachings seriously, they face misunderstanding. There is offense in the gospel! The question that we must ask as evangelical Protestant missionaries is: "If those I accompany in the faith are going to experience resistance, what can I do to ensure that it is resistance to their gospel witness and not resistance to their association with evangelical Protestantism?"

Let me warn you from the start that if you decide to minister to people in the way that I am advocating here, you will face another kind of resistance. If you begin to introduce men and women to Christ without calling them to change their religious identity, you will be resisted and opposed by *other religious leaders*! I can illustrate this from my own experience.

After we had been ministering in France for about three years I received a letter from my Director of Missions asking, "What are you doing? Are you going to start a Missionary Church, or aren't you?" In response to that question I wrote a fifteen-page letter saying, "No, we're not," and giving some reasons why.

Then our church denomination joined an evangelical association that had taken a strong stand against Roman Catholicism. When we had been in France almost ten years, they wrote to us saying, "Wait a minute! We are members of this association of evangelicals. Is what you are doing in France in line with this association's stance toward the Roman Catholic faith?" At that point I wrote a 130-page paper in which I analyzed our ministry from three perspectives: a biblical perspective, a historical perspective, and a cultural perspective. In that paper I showed that from all three of these perspectives, what we were doing was legitimate.

I am not sure that the members of missions board actually read that paper, but they called me home from the field and met with me behind locked doors on three occasions. The last of these meetings took six hours. There was tremendous opposition to our approach to the ministry in France. After lengthy, animated discussions the board was ready to take a vote on whether or not to close down their work in France, yank my credentials, etc. I was spent emotionally, so I left the room and went out into the hallway to wait for their decision.

They took their vote, after which one of the men joined me in the hall. This man had been a missionary in Africa for about twenty-five years. He said, "You know, Dave, I've never in all my experience seen such a powerful demonstration of God's ability to change human hearts as what took place right before that vote was taken." He told me that the one man who had been the most vocal in his opposition to what was happening in our ministry in France stood up and said, "I don't like what they're doing in France. I think it's wrong; but somehow I sense God is in it. And I won't vote against the Spirit of God!" So the vote was unanimous that we be allowed to continue.

People who know the Missionary Church denomination scratch their heads in amazement and say, "How in the world could they let you do what you are doing?" There is opposition. I have been banned from the pulpits of some Missionary Churches. I have received ugly, nasty letters … from pastors! I have even had letters circulated against me by individuals who feel that I should be cut off from all fellowship with evangelical Protestant believers. There is a price to be paid.

If you adopt this kind of approach to ministry in lands like France, you will also encounter the resistance of Catholic clergy and lay leaders who feel that you should not be trusted. Some of these people have had bad experiences with evangelical Protestants in the past. Others, for political reasons, do not want to reach out in a way that other Catholic leaders might not understand or appreciate. In Appendix C you can find correspondence that I had a few years ago with some of the Roman Catholic clergy who opposed my ministry because of the pressure of some Catholics who did not know me personally but who opposed the idea of having a Protestant evangelical in their midst.

No matter the road you take, you will experience opposition. If as an evangelical Protestant missionary I yank those I lead to faith in Jesus out of the Roman Catholic Church, then they receive the brunt of the opposition (as they are rejected by friends and family who see them as members of a strange cult). If as an evangelical Protestant missionary I encourage those I lead to faith in Christ to grow to spiritual maturity and service in the Roman Catholic Church, then I will bear the brunt of the opposition (as I am rejected by clergy and lay-ministers who see me as a traitor of the Reformation or a sort of

"Protestant infiltrator"). Although I am not yet able to say with the Apostle Paul, "For I could wish that I myself were cursed and cut off from Christ for the sake of my brothers" (Rom. 9:2), I do choose to be the one who faces opposition so as to not make it unnecessarily difficult for those French men and women who are turning to God (Acts 15:19).

Notes

1. (p. 100) Berkhof wrote the following pertinent remarks concerning the importance of the unity of the church as it is discussed in Scripture:

   There can be no doubt about the fact that the Bible asserts the unity, not only of the invisible, but also of the visible Church. The figure of the body, as it is found in I Corinthians 12:12-31, implies this unity. Moreover, in Ephesians 4:4-16, where Paul stresses the unity of the Church, he evidently also has the visible Church in mind, for he speaks of the appointment of office-bearers in the Church and their labors in behalf of the ideal unity of the Church. (1976:572)

2. (p. 104) In an article published in *Christianity Today*, November 7, 1986, entitled: "America's Catholics: Why Some Stay, Why Others Leave," John R. Throop, an ex-Catholic who is presently associate rector of Christ Episcopal Church, Shaker Heights, Ohio, made the following observations:

   Not every Roman Catholic has had my experience. Others have known a community of faith in the Roman church and, after coming to Christ, decided to stay. Kevin Perrotta, a member of the interfaith Word of God community in Ann Arbor, Michigan, insists that "the importance of personal faith and appropriation is genuinely part of the Roman Catholic tradition as well as the Protestant tradition. The great Catholic Reformers have always pointed to personal appropriation as a vital element of faith." In the Roman church, then, as Perrotta sees it, faith is personal and relational ... Perrotta is committed to staying in the Roman church. "I have found the Lord here," he says simply.

   Throop continues his article by writing that "many choose to stay in the Roman church because they have found God there. And many choose to stay precisely because the church is striving to become more relational and less authoritarian." Next, he quotes Bert Ghezzi, a life-long Catholic and editorial director at Strong Communications, a charismatic Christian publisher: "Popular movements are bringing Catholics to personal commitment to Christ and to personal applica-tion of Scripture." Ghezzi states that he has met few Catholics who seek to leave the church over doctrinal issues.

Nathan Hatch, a leading Protestant historian and associate dean of the College of Arts and Letters at the University of Notre Dame is quoted in the same article as saying: "The differences of doctrinal approach are important. But Protestants must remember that Catholics are Christian and some Catholics who have been reborn in the Spirit choose to stay."

Throop closes his article with this personal testimony:

> I still have points of difference with Roman Catholic teaching and practice. I cannot accept an equal pairing of the authority of Scripture and of tradition. But there are Catholics who, like me, stress the primacy of the authority of Scripture. I cannot accept the veneration of Mary. But some Catholics can't either. I cannot accept a doctrine of ministry that promotes priestly celibacy or exalted clerical hierarchy. But a lot of Catholics I know feel the same way. I believe that each person must come to a personal, saving faith in Christ. Some Catholic colleagues of mine believe that with equal passion. They stayed. I left.
>
> In most cases, relationship is a stronger factor than doctrine in decisions about staying or leaving.

3. (p. 104) Donald Bloesch has identified a number of Catholic evangelicals of both the past and present who have given to this current its present characteristics. Among those of the past he includes Richard Sibbes, the Puritan, and Philip Spener, the Pietist, who remained in their own churches to bring renewal from within. Their approach is to be contrasted with that of the radical Pietists and Separatists, who urged withdrawal from the established churches. John Wesley also sought to work for reform within his own Church of England, but the Methodist movement could not be contained within the parent body.

Bloesch also considers Count Nikolaus von Zinzendorf, P. T. Forsyth, and Philip Schaff to be included in this current. Schaff, who was associated with the Mercersburg movement, still maintained his earlier connections with the Evangelical Alliance. Unlike his colleague John Nevin, he had only kind words for John Wesley, regarding him as a preacher in the apostolic tradition (1958:815). Both Nevin and Schaff were associated with the Mercersburg movement within the German Reformed Church in North America, which sought a restoration of emphases and practices associated with the pre-Reformation Catholic tradition. The Mercersberg movement is best understood as a reaction against the rampant individualism and subjectivism in American Protestantism (Hageman 1962:97). Two other members of this group were Friedrich Heiler and Nathan Söderblom, who brought the term "evangelical catholicity" into prominence in the twentieth century.

People of our day whom Bloesch includes in the Catholic evangelical movement in its wider sense are Daniel Jenkins, Michael Green, Thomas Torrance, G. W. Bromiley, J. J. Von Allmen, J. L. Leuba, Max Thurian (the theologian of the Taizé community, a Protestant monastery in Burgundy, France), A. W. Tozer (famed preacher and spiritual writer in the Christian and Missionary Alliance, who sought to draw from the wellsprings of the Catholic mystics, whom he credits with leading him to the gospel), Klara Schlink (also known as "Mother Basilea," sister of the noted Lutheran theologian Edmund Schlink, cofounder of the Evangelical Sisterhood of Mary in Darmstadt, Germany, an evangelical convent, which brings together Reformation theology and the fervor and concerns of evangelical revivalism, including Pentecostalism [Bloesch 1974]), Max Lackmann (German Lutheran pastor, was the former head of the League of Evangelical–Catholic Reunion. For many years he maintained a close association with The Gathering [Die Sammlung] [Lackmann 1963]), Howard Hageman, Richard Lovelace (1979), John Hesselink, Robert Webber (1978), Bela Vassady (1965), John Weborg, Robert Paul, Peter Gillquist (a bishop in the Evangelical Orthodox Church and an editor for Thomas Nelson. Several of the leaders of this movement came out of Campus Crusade for Christ), and Thomas Howard. Roman Catholic scholars who are striving for an Evangelical–Catholic rapprochement include Kevin Perrotta, Stephen Clark, Ralph Martin and Kerry Koller (all related to ecumenical charismatic communities) (1983:52).

Chapter 9

Taking Dancing Lessons from the Trinity

It is amazing indeed that by the second half of the first century the closing words of the Gospel—which by general consent is the most nearly official and authoritative document of the early followers of Jesus of Nazareth—contain an unqualified injunction, stated as a command of the risen Lord Himself:

> Therefore go and make disciples of all nations, baptizing them in the name of the Father and of the Son and of the Holy Spirit. (Matt. 28:19).

This command to go and make disciples of all nations has given impetus to Christian missions through the ages and has become so familiar to the followers of Jesus that we are no longer shocked by its closing dictate to baptize new disciples in the name of the Father and of the Son and of the Holy Spirit. However, to the first century readers of the gospel these words were highly problematic.

Charles Lowry has pointed out that the phrase "in the name" does not correspond to any familiar Greek mode of expression, but was a very Jewish phrase (1946:55). The evangelist who wrote this phrase must surely have been aware of its parallelism with the holy, revered, and unutterable name of YHWH. He must have been equally aware of the sharp break with Judaism represented by including under a singular name [1] not only the Father, but also the Son and the Holy Spirit. Moreover, the evangelist was undoubtedly conscious of the association for all Jews of the "Name" with the ancient *Shema*: Hear, O Israel: The LORD our God, the LORD is one (Deut. 6:4). These observations compel us to see in St. Matthew's Trinitarian formula for baptism one of the most arresting and important phenomena of primitive Christianity. What is stunning about this baptismal formula is its inherent proclamation that Father, Son and Holy Spirit are worshipped and glorified, one God blessed forever:

> The doctrine of the Trinity is the most comprehensive and the most nearly all-inclusive formulation of the truth of Christianity. It is in and of itself a not inadequate summation of the principal teachings of the Christian religion. This doctrine is the view that the Father, the Son, and the Holy Spirit of Scripture and the Creeds and the universal continuing consciousness of the Christian Church, ever to be worshipped and glorified as distinct, individual, personal determinations and centres of Godhead, are nevertheless one God —one single, unified Divine essence or being. (Lowry 1946:77)

This chapter is about the triune nature of God and its implications for contemporary Christian missional activity in lands which have been marked by centuries of the church's presence. My belief is that reflection on the mystery of the Godhead—Trinity in Unity and Unity in Trinity—can lead us to a fuller comprehension of the missionary's role in these lands. My thesis is that a proper understanding of how the One living and true God has manifested Himself as a trinity of persons within a fundamental and absolute unity (as described by the Greek word *perichoresis*) furnishes us with a paradigm which might inform missionary endeavors in post-Christendom lands.

Numerous books and articles have been penned tracing the historical development of Trinitarian doctrine since the time of Christ. Many of these authors discuss the influence of Trinitarian thought on Christian devotion, on Christian salvation, or on Christian worship, etc. While each of these is an important area of reflection, this paper will focus on the missional implications of the Trinity.

I will refrain in this chapter from entering into the discussions concerning the highly technical language used by the church to combat the various heretical teachings that have sprung up concerning the Trinity. In fact, I will attempt to avoid all unnecessary technical theological jargon. In this chapter mine is, above all, a very practical concern: What discoveries can we make, by reflecting on the Trinity, that will enhance our missional activities in post-Christendom lands and result in greater glory to God the Father, Son and Holy Spirit?

The Missional Basis of Trinitarian Reflection

I have a friend who is fond of saying that "God had only one Son, and He was a missionary." These words reflect the fact that it is only in the context of God's "missionary" activity that the believing community has been led into the mystery of His tri-personhood. The Father sends the Son. The Son after His death and resurrection breathes upon His disciples the Holy Spirit (John 20:21) and says to them: "As the Father has sent me, I am sending you." The faith revealed in the Scriptures begins with the heavenly conceived and initiated mission of the eternal Son of God and it ends with our being sent, empowered by the Holy Spirit, to the ends of the earth.

Missionary thinkers have often reflected on the implications of the outward manifestations of the Divine Persons of the Trinity. In other words, we have looked at the Father as the One who sends both the Son and the Spirit. We have examined the Son who was sent and we have reflected on the ramifications of His incarnation. We have also studied the Person and ministry of the Holy Spirit, who was sent from both the Father and the Son. Here I will approach the missional connotations of the Trinity from a different perspective. Instead of looking at the distinctions between the Persons of the Godhead, I will be looking for lessons that can be learned from their interrelatedness. In other words, I believe missionaries working in post-Christendom lands can learn valuable lessons by examining the way in which the tri-personed God has manifested His oneness.

It was precisely in attempting to explain to non-believers the interrelatedness of Jesus of Nazareth and the Father that Trinitarian doctrine was developed. Hence, not only is the tri-personhood of God inextricably linked to His own missional activity, but history demonstrates that it has also been best understood and communicated in the context of the missionary endeavors of God's people. In his little book, *Trinitarian Faith and Today's Mission*, Lesslie Newbigin explains that when the church took the message of salvation through Jesus Christ out into the pagan world, it very soon found itself compelled to articulate a fully Trinitarian doctrine of the God whom it proclaimed:

> It is indeed a significant fact that the great doctrinal struggles about the nature of the Trinity, especially about the mutual relations of the Son and the Father, developed right in the midst of the struggle between the Church and the pagan world. ...
> The vehemence of the doctrinal struggles which centered on the formulation of the Trinitarian doctrine, and especially on the question of the relation of the Son to the Father, is evidence of the centrality of this issue for the whole Christian witness to the pagan world of that time. (1964:32)

Newbigin goes on to expound on his point by contrasting this phenomenon with what took place under the influence of Christendom.
He proposes that when the missional activity of the church subsided,
the doctrine of the Trinity did not occupy a comparable place in the
thought of Christians to what it had previously.

Beyond the missionary activity of the triune God, and beyond the
Trinitarian reflection that took place when the followers of Jesus
attempted to explain His relationship to the Father within a pagan
context, there is another reason why the missionary enterprise is the
basis for Trinitarian reflection. We find that rationale in the prayer
of Jesus recorded in the seventeenth chapter of John's Gospel:

> My prayer is not for them [those whom you gave me out of the
> world] alone. I pray also for those who will believe in me through
> their message, that all of them may be one, Father, just as you are
> in me and I am in you. May they also be in us so that the world
> may believe that you have sent me (vv. 20-21).

We will look again at these verses a little later in this study.
However, it is important at this point to notice that in this prayer Jesus
establishes His oneness with the Father as a pattern for His followers
in the context of His mission in the world.

Hence we see that reflection on the tri-personhood of God stems
from His own missionary activity, was developed in the missionary
experience of His people, and serves as a pattern, model or paradigm
for Christ's followers as they seek to communicate Him to the world.

The Need to Develop a Trinitarian Understanding of Missions in Post-Christendom Lands

The necessity for new reflection on the interrelatedness of the
Persons of the Trinity is particularly evident when one looks at the
context in which missions takes place in post-Christendom lands.

One cannot minister for Christ very long in a post-Christendom
land such as France without coming to the realization that although the
majority of people in the society have deliberately abandoned the church,
God has obedient members of His household who are very happy to
remain in the historic church of the land. This was a tremendous
revelation to me. As I shared in chapter 1, when I arrived in France
in 1979 I assumed that true followers of Christ either did not exist in
the Catholic Church, or that if they did exist, they were spiritually
weakened and compromised by their involvement in that religious

environment. I assumed that true believers in Jesus Christ could not remain practicing Roman Catholics.

This conviction, which is held by many of my evangelical missionary colleagues, leads them to try to expose the doctrinal problems which they find in the Catholic Church and call converts out of its fold. The position taken by the pioneer evangelical missionary to France and the founder of Greater Europe Mission, Dr. Robert Evans, is typical. While he is careful not to deny that there are those who are saved in the Roman Catholic Church, he goes on to say:

> The individual may indeed be saved, but if so, he has found the truth elsewhere, not in the official teaching of the Roman Church. He has learned to know Christ in a saving way not because of the church but in spite of her disapproval. Thus we should not condone the system in which this person was reared, but strengthen him to abandon it altogether in order to fully obey the Lord Jesus Christ. (1963:92)

If a Frenchman is saved, if he has learned of Christ within or even outside the Roman Church, must he be strengthened to abandon his Catholic practice in order to fully obey Christ, as Dr. Evans affirms? This and similar questions must be addressed by missionaries to post-Christendom lands: Upon what Scriptures or biblical principles can we base our argument so as to say that Jesus Christ commands a person to leave the Catholic Church? If God already has sons and daughters in the historic church, then is it really necessary for me to establish a "new church" in France? How seriously should I take the faith and witness of the ancient church in this land?

As we honestly and realistically examine the existing situation in France, we find that the members of God's household are basically divided into two camps. There exist in France "born again" members of Christ's Body, the Church, who have chosen to live, grow, and minister in what I call the "Protestant camp." Studies have shown that this group of people represents less than three percent of the total French population. The other "born again" members of Christ's Body, the Church, are those who live, grow, and minister in what I label the "Catholic camp."

What do we do with these Christian brothers and sisters? Do we ignore them or do we just pray for them? What sort of relationship does God the Father expect us to have as members of His household? Can we effectively witness for Christ if we ignore what Francis Schaeffer called "the final apologetic" (1970:138)? We have already seen the words of Jesus where He spoke of this apologetic in His prayer for the disciples: "… that all of them may be one, Father, just as you are in me and I am in you. May they also be in us so that the world may believe that you have sent me" (vv. 20-21). While we are familiar with these words we seem to have trouble knowing how to apply them.

For centuries, fellowship between the various Christian groups in France has been based primarily on conceptual, theological and organizational persuasions and practices. For this reason evangelical missionaries have not only eschewed relationships with Catholics, but have also experienced difficulties in their identification with French Protestants: "Except for a small conservative minority, French Protestant leaders traditionally maintained liberal theological principles which were anathema to evangelicals. … The missionaries kept their distance from these people" (Koop 1986:24). Even the small, fragmented French evangelical community has experienced tense relationships with the evangelical missionaries, although they share many theological persuasions and speak the same religious language, because: "The Americans were slow to realize that their work in a de-Christianized France with an ancient church initiated a novel and unique form of missionary work and often they were mystified by French evangelicals' negative reaction to their activity" (Koop 1986:26).

Contrary to our actual practice, Donald Bloesch has pointed out, one of our fundamental beliefs as evangelical Christians is that we must work to promote the unity for which Jesus prayed in John 17:

> Christian disunity is a contradiction of Christ's prayer that his people be one (John 17:20-23). It also conflicts with Paul's declarations that there is only "one body and one Spirit … one Lord, one faith, one baptism" (Eph. 4:4,5). Disunity on theological and even sociological grounds betrays an appalling ignorance of the nature of the church. Indeed, the classical marks of the church of Jesus Christ are oneness, holiness, apostolicity and catholicity. The last term denotes universal outreach and continuity with the tradition of the whole church … In my view, there will never be real evangelical unity, let alone Christian unity, until there is an awakening to the oneness and catholicity of the church. (1983:64-65)

In spite of the affirmation of the oneness and catholicity of the church, we are unsure of the nature of the unity that we should seek with believers of other Christian denominations. It is my belief that a look at the relationship between the Persons of the Trinity (described by the word *perichoresis*) can guide us as we seek to overcome some of the disunity which is still a glaring reality in our midst.

The *Perichoresis,*
The Mystery of Unity Through a Divine Dance

When theologians speak of the relationships that exist among the members of the Trinity, they sometimes use the word *perichoresis.* The most basic meaning of this word is: "a complete mutual interpenetration of two substances that preserves the identity and properties of each intact" (Harrison 1991:54). This is a fascinating concept. It contains the image of intimacy and of pure reciprocity which does not result in confusion or loss of identity. Quoting Petavius, Pohle writes:

> Perichoresis in the Godhead originates in the unity of the Divine essence, and it consists in this, that one Person cannot be divided or separated from another, but they mutually exist in one another without confusion and without detriment to the distinction between them. (1950:283)

Jesus clearly affirmed this understanding of the divine perichoresis when He said: "Believe me when I say that I am in the Father and the Father is in me" (John 14:11). This affirmation echoes Jesus' last words of public teaching where He claims that in Him people are confronted with the Father (John 12:44-50). To listen to Him is to listen to the Father; to see Him is to see the Father. In Him the Father meets people, and people meet the Father. Based on 1 Corinthians 2:11 we can expand this divine company to include the Spirit of God who knows the thoughts of God, just as the spirit of a man knows the thoughts of a man. The Apostle Paul recognized that the believer experiences through the Spirit a twofold relation: to God as Father (Rom. 8:15f.; Gal. 4:6) and to Jesus as Lord (1 Cor. 12:3).

Thus God is One in Trinity and Trinity in Unity. Pohle wrote that one of the sources of the concept of *perichoresis* is the inseparability of the Persons of the Trinity:

> The Father cannot be conceived without His Son, nor can the Son be conceived without the Father, and the Holy Ghost is altogether unthinkable without His common Spirators, the Father and the Son. St. Basil, and especially the Eleventh Council of Toledo (A.D. 675), particularly emphasized this logical aspect of the divine Perichoresis. *"Nec enim Pater absque Filio cognoscitur,"* we read in its decrees, *"nec sine Patre Filius invenitur; relatio quippe ipsq vocabuli personalis personas separari vetat, quas etiam, dum non simul nominat, simul insinuat. Nemo autem audire potest unuquodque istorum nominum, in quo non intelligere cogatur et alterum*—For neither can the Father be known without the Son, nor the Son be found without the Father; for the relation indicated by the name of a person forbids us to

separate the persons who are intimated, though not expressly named. And nobody can hear any one of these names without perceiving therein one of the others." (1950:287)

Butin uses the term *perichoresis* to understand the unity of the three Persons that focuses on their mutual indwelling or inexistence, their intimate interrelationship, and their constantly interacting cooperation (1994:161). Hill stresses that the Greek Fathers made much of *perichoresis* (literally: "dancing around") to suggest that the unity found in the Godhead is "a joyous sharing of divine life" (1982:272). He writes that "Liberty is a property of the divine nature but it is exercised only by the persons, who within the Trinity interrelate one to another in the pure creativity of uncreated freedom and love."

The teaching of *perichoresis* is that the unity of the Persons of the divine Trinity is not static. It also reveals a oneness that is more than the unity of spirit that may exist between people bound together closely in love or friendship. When they say that the Trinity relates perichoretically, theologians mean that the Three pour themselves into one another. The Father pours into the Son, the Son into the Father, and so on. Something is given to the other without which each member would not be who He is. *Perichoresis* stresses a oneness produced as each member of the Trinity is defined based upon His dynamic relationship with the other two (LaCugna 1991:270).

The Implications of a Perichoretic Understanding of the Trinity for Missions in Post-Christendom Lands

E Pluribus Unum? Can there be "one out of many" in the followers of Jesus of Nazareth today? Is the unity for which Jesus prayed only wishful thinking? If it is true that in Christ the old divisions of race and gender and even religion have been abolished (Rom. 10:12; 1 Cor. 7:19; Gal. 3:28; Col. 3:11); and if it is true that there is "one body and one Spirit … one Lord, one faith, one baptism; one God and Father of all, who is over all and through all and in all" (Eph. 4:4-6), then how can we make our unity visible?

Drawing from the perichoretic understanding of the Trinity, I propose the following guidelines for making visible the unity which Jesus has already accomplished. Remember, Jesus implied that the world would believe that He came from the Father only as His followers learned to live in the same kind of unity that is experienced in the Trinity (John 17:21).

1) Our unity is interpersonal, not organizational.

Personal contact is critical. We can read all we want about the beliefs of the other, about the decisions of Synods or Councils or their doctrinal statements, but unless we see people and talk, pray and worship the Father with them, we are not going to get very far.

Jesus lived out this perichoretic principle during His ministry on earth. Jesus carefully established and maintained an intimate relationship with God the Father. He regularly took time from His ordinary duties to go away and be alone with His Father. The Scriptures tell us that it was His habit to go away to lonely places, where He prayed (Luke 5:16; see also 6:12; 9:18, 28; 11:1; 22:41). Charles Kraft doubts that Jesus spent this time asking God for things (which is the way many of us view prayer):

> I suspect that the time was spent more relationally, perhaps discussing the events of the previous day and the plans for the next. Might much of the time have been spent simply relaxing in the Father's arms? Whatever they did, we can be sure that *they were cultivating their relationship and "feeding" their intimacy.* (1991:5)

Just as Jesus "fed his intimacy" with the Father, so we must work at developing intimacy with other members of God's family. It is only by frequent and regular time spent in friendly, intimate dialogue with our brothers and sisters in Christ that we can begin to understand the meanings that they assign to the words they use and to their religious rituals and symbols. Without this kind of deepening dialogue their perspective and interpretation of life will remain a mystery to us.

Although I recognize that it is necessary for church leaders and theologians to pursue a common understanding of the proper theological and philosophical interpretation of the symbolic and metaphorical language of the Scriptures, this is not where Christian unity is made visible to the non-believing world. [2] Personal contact and deepening relationship with Christians of other denominations allows us to discover new kinds of answers to very practical concerns: Shall we accept an invitation to teach a Catholic study group, knowing that the chances are high that they will continue to be Catholics? Or, from their perspective: If we invite this evangelical missionary to lead a catechism class or Bible study group, can we be sure that he or she will move people to deeper levels of commitment to Christ, obedience to the Scriptures, and faithfulness to our church tradition? It is only as we deepen informal interpersonal relationships with believers of other groups that more visible, formal opportunities will present themselves.

2) Our unity is to be characterized by constantly interacting cooperation.

A second principle, closely tied to the first, is that our interaction with other believers is to be one of cooperation. By this I mean that we must be willing to work together for the common end of reaching those who have not yet heard, believed, and confessed that Jesus is Lord (Rom. 10:9-15), and building up in the faith those who have (Eph. 4:11-12).

This perichoretic principle is brilliantly displayed in the Trinity, where each Person of the Divinity works together to reconcile mankind to the Creator. The Bible affirms that the Father was in Christ reconciling the world to Himself (2 Cor. 5:19), and that when Christ died for us the Father demonstrated His love (Rom. 5:8). This cooperation of the Trinity in the salvation of mankind is further demonstrated by the Holy Spirit, through whose presence the Christian experience begins (Gal. 3:2f.). In other words, one cannot belong to Christ unless one has the Spirit of Christ (Rom. 8:9), one cannot be united with Christ except through the Spirit (1 Cor. 6:17), one cannot share Christ's Sonship without sharing His Spirit (Rom. 8:14-17; Gal. 4:6f.), one cannot be a member of the Father's household except by being baptized in the Spirit (1 Cor. 12:13). Salvation has come to us through the cooperation of each of the Persons of the Trinity.

It is amazing that so few of us have recognized the importance of cooperation with other believers in our outreach for Christ. However, there are some hopeful signs that God might be leading us to a new level of involvement with one another in bringing the saving word of the gospel to others. In an article published in the Catholic ecumenical review, *One in Christ*, Thomas P. Rausch, S. J., points to several exciting recent attempts by Roman Catholics and Evangelicals to "cooperate in ways which only a few years ago would have seemed impossible" (1996:43). After examining some specific cases of advance in this area he writes:

> There are significant signs of a new and vital relationship emerging from the grass-roots. Catholics and Evangelicals share far more than a mutual interest in right to life and family values. Both remain strongly committed to the Church's evangelical mission. Both are committed to the central doctrines of the Trinity, the Incarnation, the atoning death and bodily Resurrection of Jesus. And both are concerned with a personally appropriated faith, Catholics through their emphasis on spirituality, Evangelicals through their stress on a personal relationship with Jesus.
>
> Catholics could learn a great deal about what Pope John Paul II

has called the "new evangelization," calling those no longer involved with the Church to a living sense of the faith, from Evangelical Christians. Some Catholics are beginning to take them seriously, calling for a new cooperation and learning from them. ... Evangelicals are showing a new interest in ecumenism. Some are learning to work with Catholics rather than presuming that joining a Protestant community is the only way to live a renewed life of faith. (1996:51)

He closes his article by wondering what might happen if we learned how to really cooperate in communicating the gospel to our world:

> What if the pastors of the two churches were to begin their own dialogue about the needs of their people? What if Catholic parishes or dioceses were to consider forming some of their lay ministers and evangelists in programs like Campus Crusade and Young Life? What if the growing interchange between Hispanic seminarians were to lead to a new interest in liturgical prayer and a sense for the catholicity and universality of the Church in the Evangelical pastors of tomorrow? What if Catholics and Evangelicals were to admit how much they could learn from each other? (1996:52)

What if, indeed!

3) Our unity is to preserve the identity and properties of each intact.

The perichoretic unity of the Trinity does not result in a deadening uniformity but in a diversity within unity. In His discourse to His disciples after the Last Supper, Christ clearly distinguishes between the Father and the Son and the Holy Ghost (John 19-21). In His words of comfort to His followers Jesus has already demonstrated that distinction: "I will ask the Father, and he will give you another Counselor to be with you forever" (John 14:16). This saying of the Lord so distinctly differentiates the Holy Spirit (Grk. παράκλητον "Counselor") from both Christ Himself and the Father, that a blending of the three Persons into one, or into two, is entirely out of the question. The Father "gives," the Holy Spirit "is given," and Christ "asks the Father to give" the Counselor.

The distinction between the three Persons of the divine Trinity is still more clearly marked in John 14:26: "But the Counselor, the Holy Spirit, whom the Father will send in my name, will teach you all things and will remind you of everything I have said to you." In this passage, too, it is impossible to confound the Persons of the Trinity because it is the Father who sends the Holy Spirit and it is in Christ's name that He is sent.

If our relationship with other believers is patterned after the perichoretic unity of the Trinity, then it will entail no reduction of evangelical convictions or loss of identity. Bloesch stresses that there is a place for our distinct forms of Christian witness; however that witness should always point beyond itself to Jesus Christ, the one Lord of the church to Whom all of us are subject:

> ... we need to keep alive the distinctive hallmarks of our respective traditions, but this must be done in a spirit of self-criticism and humility. We should always remember that our foremost loyalty is to Jesus Christ and that when anything in our tradition becomes more of an obstacle than an aid to the proclamation of the gospel of Christ, we must then be willing to give up what we had previously cherished. (1983:88)

4) Our unity is to build interdependence whereby each member is defined based upon his or her relationship with the others.

This is one of the most fascinating and difficult concepts expressed by the perichoretic understanding of the Trinity. We have already observed that it is impossible to understand one Person of the Trinity without reflecting on the other two.

Over and over again we see Jesus defining Himself in relationship to the Father. He says that His work is that of the Father (John 5:17, 19-23), both He and the Father have life in themselves (John 5:24-26), He pleased not Himself but the One who sent Him (John 5:30), He testified to the Father and the Father testifies to Him (John 5:37). And He claims that those who know Him know the Father also (John 8:19).

In post-Christendom lands such as France one becomes acutely aware that we cannot define ourselves apart from the other believers. Shortly after our arrival in France a friend gave us the following counsel: "Be very careful in defining your relationship toward the Catholic Church ... this seems to be a major factor determining the effectiveness of an evangelistic ministry in France." When we first received that counsel we did not realize its importance. It was not until after we had ministered for several years in France that we began to weigh its significance. Experience has shown us that our position towards Roman Catholics will determine how we are perceived by the majority of the French. This fact has been recognized by missionaries working in France since the 1960's:

> By the 1960's most missions realized that they had to achieve status in France by identifying themselves with some Christian group in French society. The missionaries never considered identifying themselves with the largest Christian group in France, Roman

Catholicism. On the contrary, their intense doctrinal opposition to Catholicism compelled them to stress their distance from Rome. (Koop 1986:171)

How difficult it is for us to apply this aspect of the perichoretic unity of the Trinity! This is particularly troublesome for us because we have become accustomed to defining ourselves in *opposition to* others, not in *relationship with* others.

Moreover, although we hate to admit it, our ecclesiological individualism is diametrically opposed to a perichoretic view of the Trinity because it leads us to believe that we do not need the others in order to be ourselves. The perichoretic view of the Trinity teaches us that we cannot define ourselves apart from the others. When this element is neglected we tend to see the others as a mere means to an end or an impediment to what we want to be or do.

5) Our unity is to consist of our pouring ourselves into the other.

Several years ago a French bishop told me that he would feel more comfortable with me if I would maintain a certain level of separateness from the Catholic world. His analysis of my ministry was: "No one that I know of can do in the diocese what you are doing. You are ministering to people that we have been unable to reach for Christ. The church is strengthened by your presence. However, Catholics and Evangelicals are like oil and water; they don't mix!"

The perichoretic understanding of the Trinity underlines the idea of intimate intermingling and involvement. It means that God intends that we would similarly pour into one another from the deepest resources of our being. One of the greatest barriers to this kind of relationship is whatever status we feel that we have "attained." Our status either makes us feel that we don't need the other, or it keeps us from giving to the other. In the first case we need to learn from the example of Jesus whose constant theme was "the Son can do nothing of himself" (John 5:19). He could have lived His life in the strength of His own divinity and thereby demonstrated His self-sufficiency. But that is not how He acted. He didn't deny His divinity, but neither did He parade it. In the second case we need to be instructed by the words and example of our Lord: "Now that I, your Lord and Teacher, have washed your feet, you also should wash one another's feet. I have set you an example that you should do as I have done for you" (John 13:14-15). We will never live out the perichoretic pouring of ourselves into the other until we are willing to strip ourselves of our ecclesiastical rights and privileges in order to serve the other (Phil. 2:5-8; 1 Cor. 9:19f.; 2 Cor. 4:5).

The Process Is the Product

The ideas that I have developed from the divine *perichoresis* are not exhaustive. I believe that meditation on this understanding of the Trinity can yield many other fruitful insights with which our ministry in post-Christendom lands might be informed.

I conclude by stressing the dynamic nature of the *perichoresis* as it is revealed in the meaning of the word itself (literally, "dancing around"). LaCugna has done an excellent job of describing this divine dance and drawing to our attention some of its implications:

> Choreography suggests the partnership of movement, symmetrical but not redundant, as each dancer expresses and at the same time fulfills him/herself towards the other. In interaction and inter-course, the dancers (and the observers) experience one fluid motion of encircling, encompassing, permeating, enveloping, outstretching. There are neither leaders nor followers in the divine dance, only an eternal movement of reciprocal giving and receiving, giving again and receiving again. To shift metaphors for a moment, God is eternally begetting and being begotten, spiriting and being spirited. The divine dance is fully personal and interpersonal, expressing the essence and unity of God as solitary. The idea of Trinitarian perichoresis provides a marvelous point of entry into contemplating what it means to say that God is alive from all eternity as love. (1991:271)

Some readers might respond negatively to this image of a dancing God. However, Murray Silberling reminds us that dance has a long and rich history as a legitimate form of Israelite worship (1995). According to Silberling, in the biblical and later Jewish traditions dance was used during religious festivals and sacred holy days to celebrate God's acts and to unite the worshipping community:

> In every culture, dance is a leading expression of community life. Each culture has historically reinterpreted dance, developing those forms and styles which meet its growing social needs. Doug Adams points out that believers have a communal tradition of sacred dance. He suggests, "surveying the Jewish and Christian records, we can see that communal rather than individual dancing is the norm for worship … there was no individual dance to God in pure Israelite practice" (*Congregational Dancing in Christian Worship* [Sharing Co., 1971] p. 6). (1995:42)

The communal nature of the Israeli circle dances coupled with the image of the divine *perichoresis* reminds us that unity with other believers, like love between people, is not a static state to be achieved.

Neither is it a product to be produced! Rather, the *perichoresis* reminds us that the process *is* the product. In other words, it is not in finally reaching consensus and agreement on doctrine, essential forms of worship, and pastoral government (as important as these things are) that we will "come to unity." Instead, it is as we interact and relate appropriately with others that we are "one."

Reactions to the Divine Dance

If we take the analogy of the divine dance even further we can, I believe, discern five types of reactions to this kind of involvement with other believers. In other words, while we might all find ourselves within the dance hall of the kingdom of God, we are not all responding in the same way to the invitation to join the dance.

Bench-Sitters

In the dance hall there are those who sit on the bench and watch other people dance. I come from a conservative evangelical Protestant church tradition that prefers to sit on the bench and avoid dancing with others. In fact, we have a tendency to condemn those who dance. We say things like: "How can so-and-so dance with those people? Isn't he aware of their background? People like us just don't get involved with folks like them." Some of these individuals view dancing as too much of a sexual temptation and they use the Bible in order to prove that dance is something that people should avoid. These people sit on the bench and judge and criticize and feel smug.

Other people sit on the bench because they have never danced before. They want to dance, but are afraid that if they get up and join in, they will make fools out of themselves. Some of those in this group of bench-sitters feel that if they can just watch others dance long enough then they will be able to learn how to dance themselves. This group of people doesn't realize that it is in dancing that one learns to dance the divine dance.

A third group of bench-sitters is comprised of those who are waiting for someone to ask them to dance. Deep inside they long to join in the divine dance but they think that no one would ever want to dance with them. Instead of realizing that they have something significant and unique to contribute to the divine dance, they refuse to take the initiative because they are afraid that they would be rejected if they took the first step.

Dance Theorists

Standing in the middle of the dance hall is a group of people I call the dance theorists. These people are listening to the music and they earnestly want to dance. However, they are very concerned that before they join in the dance they have carefully gone over all of the motions and memorized all of the choreography. So these people discuss and walk through the movements of the dance, over and over again, slowly, deliberately, until they feel that they have it "just right." Most of these people are professional dancers, and as one watches them go through the motions of the dance one is impressed that the dance will be most beautiful when they finally get around to dancing.

Solitary Dancers

In the dance hall of the kingdom there are people who are dancing. As you observe some of these dancers you notice that their motions have nothing at all to do with the movements of those around them. Theirs is a modern kind of dance that bears no similarity to the old communal types of dance. These dancers are dancing unto themselves. They hear the divine music, but they don't feel that they need the other people in the dance hall in order to dance. All that matters to these individualistically-minded dancers is their own sense of abandon and fulfillment as they respond in their own way to the rhythm of the music.

Family Dancers

Another group of dancers realizes that the divine dance is intended to be danced in relationship to others. At the same time, this group of dancers is very aware that no one dances quite the same way as those who come from one's own background. Besides, it is dangerous to dance with strangers! You can never know who you might meet on a dance floor. So this set of dancers dances with their own kind, like a brother and sister who choose to dance together rather than with those outside the family.

These dancers are dancing, but their dance simply reinforces what they already know. These individuals have the pleasure of knowing that they are no longer sitting on the bench observing others dance, and they don't run the risk of getting involved with strangers. How comfortable this kind of dance is!

Creative Dancers

Then there are those who enter into the dance with new partners.

These people enjoy the challenge of responding to the particularities that each new dance partner brings to the dance. These dancers must be attentive, alert, and able to adapt and adjust to the strengths and weaknesses that become apparent in the dancing technique of the other. In this dynamic dance each of the partners must discern when to lead and when to allow themselves to be led.

These dancers realize that they are not the ones who determine the nature of their dance, its rhythm and fluctuations. That is determined by the third member of their dance partnership, the Spirit. He is the One who binds them together and directs their steps. He is the One who indicates when they are to advance at a greater speed or slow down the rhythm. He is the One who is the most finely attuned to the music and He leads them according to its fluctuations.

It is God Himself who provides the music which gives life to the dance, and the Spirit of Christ guides us through the choreography. In this way, it is the Triune God who not only demonstrates the dance for us, but is also the One who orchestrates our movement as we seek to follow His example.

My prayer is that these reflections on my ministry in France will encourage you to learn from the Trinity how to dance the dance of love by which all people will be able to recognize that we are followers of Jesus, who was sent from the Father! (John 13:34-35; 17:21).

Notes

1. (p. 117) Joseph Pohle has observed that the essential identity of the three Divine Persons follows from the singular form *"in nomine,"* or the Greek text with its εἰς τὸν ὄνομα because throughout the Bible *"nomen Domini"* signifies God's power, majesty, and essence (1950:27-28):

   As the Three have but one name, so They have but one essence, one nature, one substance. St. Augustine beautifully observes: *"Iste unus Deus, quia non in nominibus Patris et Filii et Spiritus Sancti, sed in nomine Patris et Filii et Spiritus Sancti. Ubi unum nomen audis, unus est Deus—*This is one God, for it is not in the names of the Father, and of the Son, and of the Holy Ghost, but in the name of the Father, and of the Son, and of the Holy Ghost. Where thou hearest one name, there is one God" (August., *Tract. in Ioa.*, VI, n. 9. Browne's translation in the *Library of the Fathers*, Vol. I of the *Homilies on the Gospel according to St. John*, p. 87, Oxford 1848).

2. (p. 125) Isn't it interesting that the exact terms in which the church has formally defined the dogma of the Trinity (τριάς, οὐσία, ὑπόστασις, ὁμοούσιος) are not in the Bible; yet they express the teaching of the New

Testament which acknowledges three real Persons in one Divine Nature. God revealed His triune nature and perfect unity in temporal and spatial relationships and not in theoretical, theological or philosophical language and conceptual categories.

Appendix A

Ten Major Tendencies of French Society

What follows is translated from the book Francoscopie
by Gérard Mermet (Paris: Larousse, 1995).

1. Egology

In the 1980's the "law of the self" became increasingly more important than the "law of the collective." Each person was more and more aware that he or she was unique and attempted to express that individuality. The phrase made famous by the Three *Mousquetaires*, "One for all, and all for one," was replaced by the phrases: "Each one for himself, and everything for all," "You live only once," or "After me the Deluge." This shift ushered in the new concept of *egology*.

The French distinguish between egoism or egocentricism and *egology*. *Egology* expresses for the first time in French society not only that the individual is more important than the collective, but also that each individual is unique and complex. This word is intended to underline the autonomous nature of the individual which is seen as being more positive than individualism. *Egology* is intended to represent on a human level what *ecology* represents for the planet. Both represent a return to nature, but it is human nature that egology is to express.

> This move from a collective vision of the society to one that focuses on the individual should not be seen as a regression. It is possible that it constitutes the ultimate stage in human evolution. The era of egology is beginning. Egology, like ecology, carries within itself the seeds of a new humanism. (Mermet 1995:245)

2. The divorce between the citizen and societal institutions

The relationship between the French and their *government* has significantly degraded in the past fifteen years.

The *school system* does not have the same prestige that it held in the past.

Ninety-six percent of the French find their *justice system* to be slow, 93% find it complicated, 78% find it too costly.

The continual erosion of *church attendance* witnesses to the divorce between the French citizens and the institutionalized church: only 52% of French weddings take place in a church, compared to 84% in 1970; only 12% of French Catholics say that they regularly attend Mass, compared to 24% in 1974. Religion is no longer the reference point in questions of morality or individual behavior.

Many French men and women feel that the *trade unions* were detrimental to the overall society right from the start of the global economic crisis in the 1980's. The result is that only 1 worker in 10 is a member of a trade union today, as compared to 28% in 1981.

The *media* are severely judged by the French. Some 68% of the French feel that the television treats them like "idiots," whereas only 36% felt that way in 1986.

3. A centrifugal society

The rampant individualism of the 1980's gave birth to excesses in the social, political and economic realms of which the French have now become aware. After having been for a long time "centripetal" (naturally moving the totality of its members toward its center), French society has become "centrifugal." It tends to reject those who cannot maintain themselves in the mainstream, through a lack of education, a lack of health, or a lack of "fighting spirit." Many Frenchmen feel personally menaced by the threat of marginalization.

The reaction to this trend is beginning to be seen today. After being banished from the vocabulary of modernity, words like "morality" and "virtue" are finding an increasingly large place in public opinion. The media and intellectuals have begun using these words without fear of being seen as backward, conservative or reactionary. The majority of the French feel that the role played by morals is not important enough in today's society.

4. Democrature

Every system functions according to the relationships that are established between its parts. There are three parts that compose the social system: Actors, Media, Public.

The *Actors* are those who exercise a direct responsibility or particular influence over the social system: political parties, administrations, trade unions, major corporations, the church, public figures (artists, sports figures, research scientists). The *Public* is made up of those individuals who live within the social system (in this case, who live in France). The *Media* are the means by which communication takes place between the Actors and the Public.

Although there are many different types of relationships possible between these three parts of the social system, we can distinguish three types of society determined by which part plays the preponderant role.

When the *Actors* are controlling the society it becomes a *dictatorship*. Social relationships take place essentially from the top down (from the Actors to the Public); the Media serve to transmit the message of the Actors and are often controlled by them.

When the *Public* plays the central role in the society you have an *ideal democracy*, in which the people have the real power. Relationships take place from the bottom up, the Actors existing only to satisfy the hopes and wishes of the people.

It seems that France, along with other developed nations, has entered into a third type of social system, where the *Media* occupy the dominant place. The Media no longer are satisfied to be intermediaries between the Actors and the Public. Profiting from their enormous influence over collective life, they have now become Actors themselves. The way society functions has slowly been transformed; we have witnessed the birth of an entirely new kind of society, a "neocracy" which the French are now calling a *democrature*.

Even if the Media do not declare their ambition to manipulate public opinion, they serve to create the events they describe. It is a system that takes pride in being a counter-balance to the societal power of the Actors, yet it has been unable to develop its own counter-balance.

5. The rejection of materialism

The French are saddened by the loss or decline of certain values like politeness, honesty, justice, respect of property, family values, or human responsibility. At the same time they are less concerned about respecting traditions, honor or authority.

They denounce the importance that was placed in the 80's on material gain. Competition and an enterprising spirit are still considered good values, but it is increasingly clear that fewer and fewer of the French are willing to celebrate the "cult of performance."

One can say that, in general, materialistic and economic values are met with a growing feeling of suspicion in France.

6. Constant change

Constant change can be seen in French *shopping* patterns. The French are increasingly going from one product to another, from one shop to another, from one purchasing pattern to another (expensive/cheap, luxurious/simple, rational/irrational, specialty store/supermarket).

The French continually change their *recreational activities*, modifying their musical, sportive, and media preferences.

The French continually change in their *professional lives*, occupying successive employments according to the opportunities and obligations that they experience.

They change in their *social* and *affective lives*, changing their partners, spouses, friends, or relationships according to circumstances, incompatibilities or temptations.

They change in their *political choices* and in their *value systems*, making French society difficult to analyze.

"I change, therefore I am."

7. The end of excellence

The craze for excellence, imported into France from the United States in the 80's, first reached the business sector and then filtered down to the individual. It favored a sort of subtle dictatorship over the society. The "excellent" individual had to fit into a certain form of perfection and accomplishment characterized by youth, beauty, physical well-being, wealth, personal organization, communication skills, seduction, strength of character. To be small, obese, bald, a smoker, an alcoholic, aging, sick or luckless was seen as a grave social handicap. The individual who had an unsatisfying job, a modest salary, a small automobile or children who were struggling in school was seen as a personal failure. The dictatorship of "always more" and "always better" forced people to try to attain perfection in their professional, family, love and social lives.

This model has begun to be rejected today by many of the French. The French claim their *right to imperfection*, the possibility to pursue pleasure and to forsake constraints.

8. The rise of feminine values

There is a generalized diffusion of feminine values in French culture today. Practical sense, modesty, wisdom, intuition, balance, pacifism, gentleness and the respect for life are values that are seen as being increasingly necessary.

French industrialists have taken notice of this shift in values. French automobiles are less powerful and their form is rounder. Cameras and video recorders are at last conceived to be used by everyone, and practical products replace gadgets.

9. A new synergism

There is an obvious new attempt to observe one's surroundings with a totally open mind and to borrow certain ways of behaving, traditions or innovations from what one sees in others.

This effort to combine the elements of one's experience in such a way that their consequences exceed the sum of their individual effects can be seen in the arts. French art today finds its inspiration in other cultures, other lands and other techniques; whether it be music, painting, sculpture, literature, architecture or cinematography, the arts have become global. The French language is constantly in the process of borrowing words from beyond its frontiers to express new ideas.

The confusion of values has brought about a difficulty in distinguishing good from bad, true from false, the guilty from the innocent, nature from culture, men from women, the political left from the right, the adult from the child, work from leisure. The French are attempting to bring together these opposing concepts in a sort of *synergism* that produces something that is greater than these individual elements.

This is not an attempt at compromise between the various values. It expresses rather an attempt at reconciliation that draws economic factors closer to ecological ones, art to technology, the schools to business, science to nature, nature to culture, the useful to the agreeable, the preventative to the curative, the spirit to the body.

In this spirit new fabrics must be both resistant and light-weight. In fashion, the "chic" is no longer incompatible with sportswear, comfort with style. In food, the traditional *cassoulet* doesn't exclude the "fast food." Sick patients don't hesitate to consult both Western and Oriental doctors at the same time. Businesses attempt to be both flexible and solid. And, finally, egology (which we have already examined) attempts to reconcile the individual and the social collectivity.

10. The end of modernity

During the 60's and 70's the French were running after the ideals of modernity and postmodernity. Today, the French have the feeling that the comforts that have been brought into their lives through the scientific achievements and technological advances of modernity have diminished their *quality of life*. The growth of material comfort has produced moral discomfort. This paradox has caused many of them to question the hypotheses upon which their entire civilization has been built.

> The disappearance of certainty has corresponded to a rising sense of worry; all of the surveys taken during the past ten years witness to a general tendency of the French to consider that "things were better in the past" ... and that the worst is yet to come. Modernity and its corollary, permanent innovation, are now viewed with suspicion. (Mermet 1995:20)

Appendix B

The French and Catholicism

The following is a translation of an article published in the French Catholic magazine La Croix, *March 4, 1987, entitled "Les Français et le Catholicisme." The article is based upon a book published by the French sociologists Jean-Marie Donegani and Guy Lescanne entitled* Les Catholiques Français.

The French Catholic population poses a serious problem for sociologists: How does one explain the separation that exists between the 79% of those who call themselves Catholics and the 10% who go to Mass each weekend? Who makes up this 69% of the population? How does this group of people see themselves in relationship to the faith and the church? Religious sociology, whose function it is to count religious acts of worship and describe the external relationships between individuals and religious institutions, cannot penetrate the frontier between the conscience and deep inner motives. It is in this perspective that the work of Jean-Marie Donegani and Guy Lescanne displays its originality. Based on sixty in-depth interviews, they have come up with certain models. These models are not based upon social status or position, but rather on ways of thinking. There appear to be seven different ways in which the French view themselves in their relationship to Catholicism. This type of study does not allow us to give statistical figures, but enables us to begin to understand the inner logic behind the varying religious attitudes of the French which manifest themselves in the refusal of religious practice.

Model 1: The Consumers

The men and women who tend to fall into this category are those who organize their lives according to what they feel to be "apparent truth," without preoccupying themselves with moral, political or metaphysical considerations.

Religion for these individuals is an "apparent truth." They were born Catholic; this is a fact; they had no choice in the matter. They could just as easily have been Buddhist or Muslim. All religions have the same value, so to be Catholic is neither better nor worse than being something else. They do not revolt against their Catholic heritage any more than they resist their birth in France.

But for them religion, far from being a system of values, feelings, or an internal experience, is first and foremost rites, ceremonies and external religious observances. For these Frenchmen, the church is above all an institution whose role it is to mark the major stages of life: birth, marriage and death. They expect the church to be faithful to what she has always been and to carry out her function of dispensing religious rites without creating any sort of fuss. This is why they are upset by the recent religious reforms.

Because religion is for them a succession of rituals that tie together various generations of Frenchmen, it is best not to disturb the process.

Model 2: The Fugitives

For the fugitives, religious questions form a knot of problems from which they cannot deliver themselves. Eaten by feelings of guilt, doubt, questions and resentment, these individuals call themselves "Catholic," but no longer practice their faith.

At the heart of their religious vision live feelings of freedom and alienation. Their faith, which is permanently tied to their childhood, is associated with contradictory memories: on the one hand there are memories of tenderness, security and beauty; but there are also memories of narrowness, duty, and an impossible demand that they be perfect.

In their opinion, religion is antagonistic to happiness. One cannot, in their view of things, be Catholic and happy at the same time. This feeling is tied to their religious upbringing, which they perceive as an obstacle to personal fulfillment.

It is within this group of Frenchmen that one finds the most vehement critics of those who practice their faith and of the priests.

Model 3: The Engaged

The people who fall into this category of thinking are part of an entire social group. Those things that influence the individuals in the first two models also have influence on these folks. Their personal history is tied to the collective history of the French, which they feel is progressing towards a brighter future. They refuse an individuality which would sacrifice the collective experience.

For these individuals the world will not change all by itself. They are ready to fight for more justice and equality. Their problem: How to fight against lukewarmness, indifference and selfishness?

As long as there are hungry men and women in the world, they can't have a clear conscience. And this in the name of man and of God. They feel that the gospel is a great humanistic message. Jesus Christ is not so much the image of the Father as He is the image of man. Before one begins to try to be like Him, one must realize that He became like us.

Faith is not an exterior light that illuminates human reality. Life and faith are indissolubly united, like yeast in dough. To be Catholic is to militate for the values of justice, solidarity and sharing.

Sunday religious practice is important for some, less so for others. The most important thing for people of this model is to live their faith in some sort of social commitment. Those who find the best way to live out their faith in concrete actions are the real practicing Catholics.

Tied to this conviction is the understanding that a person cannot live his faith all alone: the gospel message is one of communal sharing. Revealed truth is less important than the sharing of experience; the experiences of the first Christians help us to understand our own experiences today.

Model 4: The Faithful

The utmost truth for this group of people is that God exists. Everything else grows out of that conviction. Only the faith can give coherence to life. To affirm one's existence is to live freely in this life and to recognize the value of the individual over and against the collective. And this is especially important in a society which has lost its points of reference and has sunk into a provisional and relativistic ethical system.

To be Catholic is to be part of a family, with all that this entails in terms of hierarchy and established order. It is in the midst of the family that we find order, solidity and identity. To be Catholic is also to hold to the Christian doctrines and practice regularly.

Those individuals who are close to this model do not speak of the humanity of Jesus, or of His contact with the humble and the sick. They speak more often of His death on the cross. For them, the light of the faith is not found inside one's self, it comes from the outside.

The people in the previous model felt that they had to create truth. For the "Faithful," truth has been revealed in history and anyone can discover it. In this model truth is to be received. Truth is a gift that is given to those who have an inner, personal experience.

In Model 5, the model of the "Fraternal," truth is neither created nor received, because it already exists in each of us. This truth is discovered by simplifying one's lifestyle.

The "Faithful" experience a great deal of fear as they witness the evolution of the church: they are afraid that the tolerance and openness to others will empty Catholicism of its substance. One could perhaps treat these individuals as retrogrades; this does not bother them. They simply remind you that the crucified Christ was Himself misunderstood.

Model 5: The Fraternal

This group is made up of the youngest segment of those in our study. Believers who sometimes practice their faith, they do not want to be confused with the traditional, practicing Catholics.

Ever since their youth, these individuals have been involved in the catechism and in various youth movements of the church. They witnessed post-Vatican II tensions between the "Engaged" and the "Faithful." And they are partly a result of those conflicts.

They say that they have discovered how to simplify their lives and follow an interior voice which has taught them how to live and believe "differently."

More Christian than Catholic, they feel very uncomfortable in situations where they feel pressed into a mold. In their youth they bathed in a climate of religious certainty. They have separated themselves somewhat from those former experiences, but they have a fervent belief in God, in life and in love.

They are looking for new ways to reappropriate their religious traditions. They are suspicious of grandiose visions of the world, and feel that one need not be an intellectual to live the gospel. Religion, for them, is daily life.

They see Christ as the example of respect, of compassion and love. He was with the poor and the despised.

Respect for others and tolerance are the essential values to which this group of people cling. They do not allow for any exceptions. They see Christ in others, especially in the poor and those on the fringes of society. If the "Faithful" speak the most often of the family, the "Fraternal" speak of the community. It is among others that they seek to find their identity.

Model 6: The Indifferent

These individuals live a peaceful search without inner turmoil or conflict. This is the source of their strength and balance. They are unwilling to receive anything from anyone else.

Although they have received a religious education, they rebel at the idea of being at the mercy of any particular religious system. For them, no religion or culture can pretend to occupy a central position.

Religion cannot provide them with truth. They seek to discover truth within themselves. It is important that the individual can be fully himself without the help of any support system.

Model 7: The Cultural

All of the people in this spiritual family were reared in a social Catholicism, and their world view is influenced by that heritage.

However, they are all slowly and serenely separating themselves from that past. Although they recognize their Catholic origin, the "Cultural" don't want to be implicated in any of the do's or don'ts of religion.

They feel that they have been indelibly marked by religion, yet desire that their religious experience not influence all aspects of their behavior. They prefer that religion be one compartment of their lives among others.

They recognize that the religious dimension exists, that it is a trait of humanity, yet it should not influence their present experience. They are bothered by moral absolutes and codified dogma. For them, Christianity is one of many dimensions of human culture.

Appendix C

Incarnational Ministry on Trial

What follows are English translations of some of the correspondence which I exchanged a few years ago with the Roman Catholic bishop and other Catholic leaders in the area of France where I was ministering. At the time the bishop was reacting neither to my teaching nor to my methods, but was drawing back from previous positive statements concerning my ministry to a more conservative view because of the opposition of some individuals who did not know me at all, but who felt that evangelical Protestants should be kept outside the Catholic fold.

The correspondence should enable you to understand the climate of my relationship with these Catholic leaders at its worst. This was a very painful and difficult time for me, for my wife and children, for the French people we had accompanied in the faith, and for the missionaries who ministered with me in France.

from the Bishop of ...   June 22, 1992

to Mr. David Bjork
   Mr. ...

Sirs and dear friends,

I wish to thank you for the time which you set aside to meet with me, in all confidence, this morning in —. We admit that the meeting became progressively less stressful as we conversed this morning the 22nd of June 1992.

We came to the agreement that your relationship to the Catholic Church, in the Diocese of — and in terms of collaboration, would be lived out exclusively in the town of —, and within the exclusive framework of the parish of —, and this with a maximum of discretion.

Consequently, you will no longer intervene, beginning in September of 1992, and during two years, up to the 31st of August 1994, except as members of that community which meets together, prays and fellowships.

You will no longer have the responsibility of preparing individuals to receive the sacraments. You will no longer be given the role of preparing for Confirmation. That role will henceforth be given to a group of Christians in the parish, who will operate under the direct and permanent responsibility of a priest. The propositions that could be made to those young people who receive the sacrament of Confirmation, with the goal of deepening their faith, will also be submitted directly to the ordained ministers of the Catholic Church.

You may see yourselves as members of that parish community, without accepting any delegated role, whether it be on the Parish Pastoral Council, within the context of Catechism classes, or in the propositions of spiritual training.

To the extent that you continue your Bible studies, it must be clear for all of the Catholic participants at these meetings, which take place on Tuesdays, that your intervention is in the name of your Protestant uniqueness. So that the tie with the Catholic Church establishes itself with clarity, I have decided that the Father —, chaplain on the University campus, participate each month at these Tuesday night meetings, in his role as a Catholic priest. This ministry could not be given to any of the priests who are presently working in the parish in —, for the reasons which I mentioned this morning in our conversation.

You will maintain your ties of friendship and ecclesiastical accompaniment, discernment and evangelical questioning with the Father —. You will contact the Father —, who is responsible for ecumenism in the diocese. He will have the mission of preparing an institutional meeting with those partners with whom we have an already established and approved ecumenical dialogue.

The meetings with the Bishop of — will take place each trimester, following a schedule which we will establish, beginning in September of 1992.

This letter constitutes a sort of moratorium, as we have agreed. It should help to calm certain individuals, liberate us from categorical judgments and deepen the base for a better dialogue. We will strive to avoid all forms of missionary syncretism. We will work to avoid all smoothing out of our differences and the silencing of our divergences, in the name of a spontaneous turning to the Spirit to whom we are, as it were, directly tied through our spiritual experience or our good will.

Since I feel it necessary, because of my ministry in this particular church of Catholic tradition, to present you with these decisions, in the name of the truth which sets free, and in the hope that you can accept these conditions, I ask that you accept, dear friends, my cordial feelings of brotherhood and devotion in the Lord.

signed

Bishop of —

I responded to this letter on the 30th of June:

Monsignor and dear friend,

I wish to thank you for the welcome that you reserved for the pastor — and myself on Monday the 22nd of June. We are very sensitive to the difficulties which you encounter because of our presence in the midst of those Catholic communities where we have been ministering until now.

I am writing to you today with the goal of assuring myself that we have correctly understood the meaning of your letter from the 22nd of June which describes our relationship to the Catholic Church in the diocese of —. In your second paragraph you state: "We came to the agreement that your relationship to the Catholic Church, in the Diocese of — and in terms of collaboration, would be lived out exclusively in the town of —, and within the exclusive framework of the parish of —, and this with a maximum of discretion." Could you permit me and my family, along with the pastor — and his family, to attend Mass in those parishes where we are presently living rather than limiting us to the parish of —? We understand clearly that we must limit our involvement to simply attending Mass for our own personal edification, and with a maximum of discretion.

We understand clearly that we will no longer be preparing individuals to receive the sacraments. We are certain that our preparation of the young people was in every way in agreement with the demands of the Catholic Church. Rev. — and myself have taken courses at the Catholic Seminary in — for a number of years with the goal of being sure that the preparation which we offered to these young people was correct. Those whom we prepared see themselves as Catholics, committed Christians, disciples of Jesus Christ, witnesses to the gospel, members of the church. It is our understanding that you are withdrawing from us the right to prepare individuals to receive the sacraments, not because we have betrayed the gospel or the church, but because you wish that Catholics take this responsibility.

Your sentence: "The propositions that could be made to those young people who receive the sacrament of Confirmation, with the goal of deepening their faith, will also be submitted directly to the ordained ministers of the Catholic Church" is problematic for us. We understand by that sentence that you want us to quit accompanying those young people in the faith. If this is indeed your wish we will submit, but you are creating in us a deep wound and conflict. We have been following these young people for a number of years and we love them as if they were our own children. We are praying that you will grant us the freedom to continue on with these young people and their families.

If you don't change your position, we will inform those teenagers of your decision by letter in the month of September. We will write to them that you wish for us to quit accompanying them in their faith because we are not Catholic. We will state specifically that you have found nothing wrong with our teaching or in our behavior. If they say that they don't care what you think and that they want to continue on with us, we will tell them to discuss that with you. We refuse to do anything with them that would go against your decision.

As concerns the Bible studies that take place in the parish of —, we have never hidden from the Catholic participants in those studies that we are Protestant pastors. We have stated to them that we are "Protestants serving the Catholic Church." I sincerely regret the ambiguity which accompanies this kind of pastorate. The Apostle Paul must have lived in the same kind of ambivalence when he made himself a "slave of all," in order to win as many as possible. The Judeo-Christian communities must have struggled as they attempted to understand him who acted as if he were free from the law so as to win those not having the law. This same Apostle must have been a missionary whom some converts from a pagan background just couldn't stomach as they watched him become like one under the law, so as to win those under the law. In spite of the difficulties of comprehension, and the sectarian attitudes which dominate, isn't the apostolic position one of becoming all things to all men so that by all possible means we might save some? (1 Cor. 9:19-23).

We accept that the Father —, Chaplain on the University campus, participate each month at these Tuesday night meetings, in his role as a Catholic priest. Jesus Christ whom we serve is our witness that we have never sought to harm the Catholic Church, neither in her hierarchy, nor in her Christian traditions. We will continue to live with the Catholic participants at these Bible studies as we have the custom of living together.

I wish to thank you for allowing us to maintain our ties of friendship and ecclesiastical accompaniment, discernment, and evangelical questioning with the Father —. We will contact the Father —, who is responsible for ecumenism in the diocese, according to your wishes.

It is with a great joy that we will meet with the bishop of — each trimester. We pray that these meetings will allow us to better know and understand each other for the greatest good of the church.

We are not sure that we understand correctly the entire meaning of the next to last paragraph of your letter from the 22nd of June. By your sentence, "We will work to avoid all smoothing out of our differences and the silencing of our divergences, in the name of a spontaneous turning to the Spirit to whom we are, as it were, directly tied through our spiritual experience or our good will," we understand that you wish to underline what divides and separates us rather than what we share in Christ. If that is the meaning of your sentence aren't you in disagreement with 1 Corinthians 12:13 which describes the entrance of an individual into the Body of Christ: "For we were all baptized by one Spirit into one body—whether Jews or Greeks, slave or free, [Catholics or Protestants]—and we were all given one Spirit to drink"? In the Gospel of John (13:34-35 and 17:20-23), doesn't Jesus undeniably teach that the church should be undivided? Wasn't it the teaching of the church fathers as well during the first century that the church should be one and universal? And what should we make of the exhortations of the Apostle Paul addressed to the church at Ephesus: "Make every effort to keep the unity of the Spirit through the bond of peace. There is one body and one Spirit (just as you were called to one hope when you were called), one Lord, one faith, one baptism; one God and Father of all, who is over all and through all and in all." We understand the words of Vatican II to be saying this same thing: "It is necessary that Catholics recognize the joy and appreciate the truly Christian values which have their origins in the common patrimony which is that of

our separated brothers" (Decree *Unitatis Redintegrato,* The Catholic
Principles of Ecumenism).

We know that the wealth of what we share in Christ goes far
beyond all that could present a barrier between us Protestant pastors
and you Catholic priests. If God the Father calls you His son, and calls
me His son, then we must learn to live together as brothers even if
we don't totally agree on every point of doctrine or procedure. What
is at stake is not who is right and who is wrong. What is truly at stake
is finding how we can work together so that the greatest number of
French men and women enter into a personal knowledge of God
(John 17:3). The real issue is love, love that covers over divisive
differences. If we separate from you because of some point of detail,
wouldn't that mean that our love for our own opinions is greater
than our love for you, our brother? And how could we possibly
evangelize the French when we are preoccupied by our differences
(John 13:34-35)?

The Apostle Paul stated that we must have the same love, being
one in spirit and purpose: "strive after unity; do nothing out of selfish
ambition or vain conceit … but in humility consider others better than
yourselves. Each of you should look not only to your own interests,
but also to the interests of others. Your attitude should be the same as
that of Christ Jesus" (Phil. 2:3-11). In order to live according to these
Scriptures we have left our country, our families, and our Christian
environment. We have been forced to give up our right to celebrate
the sacraments as do other Protestant pastors and Catholic priests.
We don't receive the respect which is given to others who are ordained
members of the Church of Jesus Christ. The Catholic hierarchy looks
at us with suspicion while, at the same time, we are misunderstood
in the midst of our own church in the United States of America.

When Catholic leadership in various parishes or at — asked us to
help them, we did it with our whole heart. We prepared ourselves,
like simple laymen at the Catholic seminary in — in order to be
certain that we didn't betray the trust of those individuals we were
called to serve.

Today you ask us to limit even more our evangelical action.
We left — where for the last five years I have given two days a week
serving the gospel, serving the church, and serving the teens. I leave
— with a lot of pain, but I obey you.

You have asked that Rev. — leave his ministry within the parish
of —. Rev. — has been working in the parish for the last eight years,
serving Christ, serving the parish priests, serving on the Pastoral

Council, and serving the youth of the parish. No one can question his integrity or his commitment. Today you ask him to leave what he has been building in Christ's name for eight years, and he is doing it amidst much pain, but he is obedient to you.

We hope, Monsignor —, that together we can build bridges between Christians in the diocese of — and that we can destroy the walls that hide from human eyes the beauty of Christ. In the hope that you understand the spirit of our evangelical action and our willingness to submit ourselves to your ministry within the particular church of Catholic tradition, I ask that you accept our friendship in the Lord.

signed

Rev. David Bjork

On the 28th of July the bishop replied to my letter of June 30:

Bishop of —   July 28, 1992

Dear friend,

Your letter from the 30th of June, in the prolongation of our meeting and the letter which prompted your correspondence, merits in effect, some clarifications and commentary.

You will allow me, without holding me to the letter of what I write, to bring up some of the elements which seem very important to me today:

Page 1, paragraph 2, line 4: Your relationship to the Catholic Church in the Diocese of —, will take place henceforth, in an intervention strictly limited to the unique Catholic community of — which meets at —. Do not give to my intentions or to my text another extension. Christians who live differently by participating in meetings in other parishes do so on their own private initiative, and I cannot impose limits on them. You will note that you will satisfy yourselves with simple attendance at Mass for your own personal edification.

Page 2, paragraph 1: I maintain my decision for strict reasons tied to the coherence of the Catholic faith. I prefer, today, to provoke the wound in you to which you refer in your letter. It seems to me to be more conformed to the Catholic way of doing things to give that preparation, follow-up and accompaniment to ordained representatives of the Catholic Church. You can write to those young people informing them of the position which I feel to be best today.

Before I would receive those young people, it seems to me, that the position of the bishop of — should be explained, admitted and accepted within the pastoral context. I have had the opportunity to remind you sufficiently that the life of a Christian community does not express itself, to begin with, in its relationship to the hierarchy, but rather in a base relationship of fellowship. It is with the clergy of the town of — that these youth should dialogue in order to enter into an understanding of the dispositions taken by the bishop of —.

In your paragraph 3: I think that it would have been better had you specified that you are a particular type of Protestant, without ties to the Reformed Church, inserted *without mandate* into a Catholic community, *more than in service* to the Catholic Church. Had you presented yourselves in this way you would have avoided all ambiguity and probably would have invited the partners of your meetings to ask themselves a certain number of questions.

The reference to Father — is not in the least based upon my suspicion of the priests in —, but rather on the desire of someone who is responsible, to obtain by a priest who is outside of what has been practiced, experienced and decided, information which will allow me to situate myself more freely.

The references to 1 Corinthians 12:13 correspond to a way of quoting Scripture which disconnects it from the Tradition of the Church, which is my point of reference, and does not correspond with our way of proceeding. You do not ever make a precise reference to that Tradition which is for us the passageway, the explanation and the clarification of our relationship to Scripture.

Moreover, as I expressed to you in written form, and without doubt verbally, I am continuing, of course, to gather information about your church through my contacts with the American bishops, so as to be able to clarify the evolution of our relationship because of the still unanswered questions in the midst of the collaboration defined by my recent letter.

I understand that these exchanges are painful and provoke a certain shock for you. It seems more true to me to maintain these dispositions.

Counting on your spiritual comprehension, I ask that you accept, dear friend, my cordial feelings of brotherhood and devotion in the Lord, accompanied by my prayer.

signed

Bishop of —

The following letter expresses my reaction to these words of the bishop:

Father —   September 9, 1992

Dear friend,

   I am writing to you today in order to send you a copy of the letter which I received from Monsignor — in response to my correspondence from the 30th of June. I have also decided to share with you my reactions to his letter rather than to write to him directly seeing that he has given you the task of accompanying us in our ecclesiastical discernment.

   First, I want you to know how much we appreciate the time you set aside for us. Your friendship, your perspective on the nature of the Catholic Church, your evangelical judgment, and your courageous integrity are of an inestimable value to us in our proceedings. We think that it is wonderful to be able to express to you our questions, disappointments and frustrations with the traditionally Catholic world without fear of surprising you or losing the fellowship we share because of Christ.

   I would like to respond in the name of the missionary team of World Partners in France (and in the name of the thousands of Christians in the United States of America, from the Christian community which sent us to France thirteen years ago), to the paragraph of the bishop's letter which discussed how we have presented ourselves in France. I feel that the bishop is incorrect in stating: "I think that it would have been better had you specified that you are a particular type of Protestant, without ties to the Reformed Church, inserted *without mandate* into a Catholic community, *more than in service* to the Catholic Church. Had you presented yourselves in this way you would have avoided all ambiguity and probably would have invited the partners of your meetings to ask themselves a certain number of questions."

   First, it seems that the bishop is reproving us for *infiltrating* ("inserted without mandate") a Catholic community without sufficiently explaining our position as "a particular type of Protestant," which apparently means, for him, not from the traditional Reformed Church. Apparently, he feels that had people realized who we really are they would have been slowed down in their willingness to relate to us through their normal suspicion. This accusation is completely wrong for a number of reasons! You can ask those responsible Catholics in the communities where we have ministered their opinion. This remark of the bishop does not apply to our situation first of all because we have always stated clearly that we have no ties with the Reformed Church and we gave the priests and other Catholic leaders written explanations concerning the nature of the Missionary Church, concerning her history, her convictions, her goals, concerning the gospel message that we preach, and concerning the missionary work of the Missionary Church. Moreover, we did not *infiltrate* Catholic structures; we have only ministered in places where the ordained leadership of the Catholic Church has asked us to do so.

Added to these remarks, I contest the words of the bishop when he says that we are *without mandate, more than in service* to the Catholic Church. We have received a mandate for our ministry which comes directly from Christ; that mission is confirmed by the Holy Scriptures and by the Christian community which ordained us and sent us out with the laying on hands. What does this mission consist of? 1) The proclamation of the gospel of Jesus Christ, leading men and women to Christ and grouping them together into apostolic communities using methods adapted to the French culture. 2) Assuring that the members of these communities grow in their faith and become workers who work effectively for Christ in their church, the Roman Catholic Church. 3) Help some of the members of these communities to take the responsibility for the community, or help them to begin other communities throughout France and the French-speaking world. *It is precisely because we received this mandate that we say that we are serving the Catholic Church and are submitting today to the directives of Monsignor —!*

It seems to me that the Father — is really questioning the *reasons* for our desire to serve the Catholic Church (he suspects some hidden agenda). It seems clear to us that the Father — is trying to situate us. I don't know if the research he is doing among the American bishops will bring the responses he hopes to obtain. We belong to the evangelical Protestant world, and that world does not practice an official, recognized ecumenism. However, thousands of evangelical Protestants experience an active ecumenism with their neighbors and friends in the dioceses in the U.S.A. Perhaps the bishop will decide that he prefers that we leave the Catholic world and join the Protestant evangelical world, not wanting to practice ecumenism with Christians like us. Even if the Father — took such a stance, in two years, we would continue to do our work of evangelism and follow-up without starting a Protestant church or community.

The reaction of the bishop to my way of quoting the Scriptures surprises me. The fact that we look to the Word of God to find the meaning of our missionary call, without looking to the Traditions of the Catholic Church for our point of reference, clarification and explanation, seems to be highly displeasing to our bishop. I am sorry if our way of reading and understanding the Holy Scriptures irritates him. There is not much that we can do to change that; this is one of the areas that distinguishes the Catholic and Protestant churches. The way we approach the Holy Scriptures is a fundamental point of divergence which we will have to discuss further.

The Christians who are the product of our ministry are a little bit particular. They believe that the Second Vatican Council was right to exhort *"with force* and in a *special way* all Christians to obtain through frequent readings of the Holy Scriptures 'an imminent knowledge of Jesus Christ' (Philippians 3:8), for 'ignorance of the Scriptures is ignorance of Christ'" (Vatican II, Dogmatic Constitution on Divine Revelation (*Dei Verbum*), Chapter 6, 25). It is in the discovery of the Bible that these individuals have discovered Christ. That is why they draw near to the Sacred text with their whole hearts during our meetings. This way of approaching the Holy Scriptures does not keep them from being good Catholics, as the testimony of F— (which I am enclosing with this letter) clearly shows.

I hope that this letter helps you to understand us. We are anxious to see you again and to be able to discuss these things face to face.

Your brother in Christ,

signed

David Bjork

from F —

Dear David,

I appreciate the confidence with which you shared with me the difficulties encountered in the diocese of — by the pastoral action of the evangelical missionary team for which you are responsible. The situation seems to be truly complex, and I hope that the time of discretion which is demanded of you by Monsignor — will allow each one to weigh and evaluate correctly the various questions which have been raised: pastoral, doctrinal and relations. I hope that this time allows each one to discern and look for solutions which will contribute to the growth of the kingdom of God.

I would like, during this period when your choices for the Lord are put to the test, to tell you in all freedom what an important role your choices have played in my life, the fruits that I see to your action, the questions which your action unavoidably must raise, and how, in my opinion, the moratorium period should be put to profit.

You know that I have had a living encounter with Jesus Christ through the testimony of our friend C— which I heard when I was a university student in —. C— had been himself previously touched by your proclamation of the gospel. Up to that point in my life I had not had the occasion to hear the words of our Lord except during the catechism classes which preceded my First Communion. My First Communion signaled for me, as is the case for many of my generation in this land, the end of all formal relationship with religion. But beyond the testimony of C—, it is the words of Christ which gave me the desire to meet him: "If anyone hears my voice and opens the door, I will go in and eat with him, and he with me," says the Amen in the book of Revelation. I didn't resist the desire, and for the nine years since I opened my heart to the Lord, I can say that my life has taken on meaning and worth. In that foundation experience I recognize the characteristic workings of the Spirit which he has been doing since the beginnings of the church, for as the Apostle states "faith comes through hearing, and hearing through the Word of God."

Ever since my conversion, through my progression in the Catholic Church, going from my involvement in the Christian student movement at the University of Paris-XI to my involvement in the Christian life movement, where for the last three years I have been helped by the spirituality of the Jesuits, and passing by way of the diocese of St. Pierre and Miquelon and the diocese of Le Mans, during this entire pilgrimage I have received inestimable spiritual help from you and your team in —.

I am indebted to you for pushing me to rediscover my Catholic identity, for having given me hunger and respect for the Scriptures which are for me today the source of spiritual life; I am indebted to you for helping me to understand, through the Bible studies which we have done together and through the witness of your lives, a number of spiritual realities upon which I am building my life each day. I am indebted to you for your example which has given me a heart conviction concerning the importance and the urgency of reaching out with the gospel. During times of difficulty I have found the warm welcome of godly friends, and in terms of my spiritual training which enables me to "stand firm" in the faith, you are, David, one of the three or four people who has helped me the most.

Truly, your evangelistic action has been the catalyst in my meeting the Lord, in my commitment to the Word of God, in my love for the Catholic Church, and in one part of my spiritual training. Of course, I have found in the variety of that Church other riches for which I give thanks.

I am not the only person who has benefited from the grace of the Lord distributed through your mission: I have seen your action bear fruit according to the gospel in the lives of H—, E— and C—, S— and J—, and many other Catholics who are quite active in the church.

David, you know my feeling for the Catholic Church. You know that I love the church to the point that I am discerning with my Jesuit friends whether or not I should consecrate my life in full time ministry in the church. You know as well that the questions that the church is asking today do not surprise me. I understand her difficulty in trying to identify who you are. Your mission is absolutely unique. I think, personally, that the real questions lie in the recognition of your teaching and pastorate, which is done within the Catholic Church but outside her hierarchy and without a ministry which she gives to you, for the reasons tied to your Protestant confession and the structures that support your mission. At the same time that I believe the Lord to be at work through you, I ask myself these same questions, and I know of no answers today. I don't think that the time is ripe.

That is why I think that the moratorium period which is beginning should be used for two things: the bishop of — should get to know you better and see for himself the fruits of your ministry in order to be able to judge clearly, and a study should be done within the church to define a place where she can welcome and support your action while remaining true to her Canon law. I think that your obedience to Monsignor — is the best proof that you really wish to serve the Catholic Church.

I want to assure you, David, of my support in the name of the brotherly ties which unite us, and of my prayers for the future of your mission.

signed

F —

References

Aldrich, Joseph C. (pp. 28, 30)
  1981 *Life-Style Evangelism*. Portland: Multnomah.
Andersen, Wilhelm (p. 64)
  1955 *Towards a Theology of Mission*. London: SCM.
Ardagh, John (p. 35)
  1982 *France in the 1980's*. New York: Penguin.
Atallah, Ramez L. (pp. 64, 103)
  1974 "Some Trends in the Roman Catholic Church Today," in *Let the Earth Hear His Voice: Official Reference Volume; Papers and Responses, International Congress on World Evangelization*. J. D. Douglas, ed. Pp. 872-84. Minneapolis: World Wide Publications.
Babcock, Bruce (pp. 33, 34, 50)
  1988 "A Light in the Night in France," *OMS Outreach* 87, 5 (September-October): 1-6.
Banks, Robert (p. 89)
  1994 *Paul's Idea of Community*. Peabody, MA: Hendrickson.
Bassham, Rodger C.
  1979 *Mission Theology: 1948-1975, Years of Worldwide Creative Tension —Ecumenical, Evangelical, and Roman Catholic*. Pasadena: William Carey Library.
Bayssat, Françoise, Donna Brenneman and Jim Renick (p. 99)
  1986 "Chicago Consultation on Partnership in Western Europe" (December). Organized by World Mission Associates European Project, Lancaster, PA.
Bedard, Bob (p. 24)
  1996 *Evangelization: A Challenge for the Catholic Church*. Ontario: Catholic Renewal Centre in Ottawa.
Beeby, Dan H. (p. 18)
  1994 "A White Man's Burden, 1994," *International Bulletin of Missionary Research* 18, 1: 6-8.

Berkhof, Louis   (p. 114)
  1976   *Systematic Theology*. Edinburgh: Banner of Truth.

Beyerhaus, Peter   (p. 68)
  1979   "The Three Selves Formula: Is It Built on Biblical Foundations?"
        In *Readings in Dynamic Indigeneity*. Charles H. Kraft and Tom N.
        Wisley, eds. Pp. 15-29. Pasadena: William Carey Library.

Billheimer, Paul E.   (pp. 4-5)
  1981   *Love Covers*. Fort Washington, PA: Christian Literature Crusade.

Black, David Alan   (p. 13)
  1995   (1988) *Linguistics for Students of New Testament Greek*. Grand
        Rapids: Baker.

Blauw, Johannes
  1962   *The Missionary Nature of the Church*. New York: McGraw-Hill.

Blocher, Louis   (p. 62)
  1966   "Mission and Proselytism," in *The Church's Worldwide Mission*.
        Harold Lindsell, ed. Pp. 111-23. Waco, TX: Word.

Bloesch, Donald G.   (pp. 10, 105, 106, 115-16, 122, 128)
  1974   *Wellsprings of Renewal*. Grand Rapids: Eerdmans.
  1983   *The Future of Evangelical Christianity: A Call for Unity Amid Diversity*.
        Garden City, NY: Doubleday.

Boon, J. Edward   (p. 69)
  1982   "Will the Barriers Be Broken?" *The Alliance Witness* (November):
        5-19.

Brown, Harold O. J.   (p. 103)
  1976   "Contemporary Dialogues with Traditional Catholicism," in
        Theology and Mission. David Hesselgrave, ed. Pp. 147-60. Grand
        Rapids: Baker.

Bruce, Alex B.   (p. 71)
  1955   *The Humiliation of Christ*. Grand Rapids: Eerdmans.

Butin, Philip Walker   (p. 10, 124)
  1994   *Revelation, Redemption and Response*. New York: Oxford University
        Press.

Carrier, Hervé   (p. 56)
  1993   *Evangelizing the Culture of Modernity*. Maryknoll: Orbis.

Clark, Stephen   (p. 77)
  1972   *Building Christian Communities: Strategy for Renewing the Church*.
        Notre Dame, IN: Ave Maria Press.

Clinton, J. Robert and Richard W. Clinton   (p. 87)
  1991   *The Mentor Handbook: Detailed Guidelines and Helps for Christian
        Mentors and Mentorees*. Altadena, CA: Barnabas Publishers.

Cragg, Kenneth (p. 38)
1956 *The Call of the Minaret*. London: Lutterworth.

Dawe, Donald G. (p. 71)
1963 *The Form of a Servant: A Historical Analysis of the Kenotic Motif.* Philadelphia: Westminster.

Dawson, Christopher (pp. 16, 23, 24)
1965 (1960) *The Historic Reality of Christian Culture*. New York: Harper.

de Benoit, Alain
1981 *Comment peut-on être païen?* Paris: Albin Michel.

Donegani, Jean-Marie and Guy Lescanne (pp. 141-45)
1988 *Les Catholiques Français*. Paris: Desclée-Bayard Press.

Edgar, William (p. 15)
1983 "New Right—Old Paganism: Anatomy of a French Movement." Published in English in *Nederlands Theologisch Tijdschrift* 37, 4: 304-13.

Edman, V. Raymond (pp. 14, 23)
1949 *The Light in Dark Ages*. Wheaton: Van Kampen Press.

Elliott-Binns, L. E. (p. 14)
1957 *The Beginnings of Western Christendom*. Greenwich, CT: Seabury.

Ellul, Jacques (pp. 34, 43)
1986 "What You Need to Know About France in Order to Serve God More Effectively There," *World Pulse* 21, 23.

Erickson, Millard J. (pp. 71, 75)
1991 *The Word Became Flesh*. Grand Rapids: Baker.

Erickson, Norman R. (p. 41)
1978 "Implications from the New Testament for Contextualization," in *Theology and Mission*. David Hesselgrave, ed. Grand Rapids: Baker.

Evans, Robert P. (pp. 34, 121)
1963 *Let Europe Hear*. Chicago: Moody.

Forsyth, P. T. (p. 81)
1909 *The Person and Place of Jesus Christ*. Boston: Pilgrim Press.

Franklin, Kris (p. 74)
1997 "How I Solved the Catholic Problem," *Envoy Magazine*, Premiere Issue, pp. 29-36.

Getz, Gene A. (p. 79)
1974 *Sharpening the Focus of the Church*. Chicago: Moody.

Good, Kent (p. 40)
1986 *Grace Magazine*, Special Europe Missions Issue. 2, 1 (Winter).

Gore, Charles (p. 81)
  1889 "The Holy Spirit and Inspiration," in *Lux Mundi*, 5th ed. Charles Gore, ed. Pp. 299-302. New York: John W. Lovell.
Gunton, Colin E.
  1993 *The One, the Three and the Many: God, Creation and the Culture of Modernity.* Cambridge: Cambridge University Press.
Hageman, Howard G. (p. 115)
  1962 *Pulpit and Table.* Richmond: John Knox.
Harrison, Verna (p. 123)
  1991 "Perichoresis in the Greek Fathers," *St. Vladimir's Theological Quarterly* 35, 1: 53-65.
Hébrard, Monique (p. 77)
  1987 *Les Nouveaux Disciples Dix Ans Après.* Paris: Le Centurion.
Heidman, Eugene P. (p. 97)
  1996 "Proselytism, Mission, and the Bible," *International Bulletin of Missionary Research* 20, 1: 10-12.
Hendricks, Howard G. (p. 87)
  1995 *As Iron Sharpens Iron: Building Character in a Mentoring Relationship.* Chicago: Moody.
Henrichsen, Walter A. (p. 85)
  1974 *Disciples Are Made—Not Born.* Wheaton: Victor Books.
Herrmann, Siegfried (p. 20)
  1981 *A History of Israel in Old Testament Times.* London: SCM.
Hesselgrave, David J. (pp. 86, 93, 96, 97)
  1978 *Theology and Mission.* Grand Rapids: Baker.
  1980 *Planting Churches Cross-Culturally.* Grand Rapids: Baker.
  1982 *Communicating Christ Cross-Culturally.* Grand Rapids: Baker.
  1988 *Today's Choices for Tomorrow's Mission.* Grand Rapids: Zondervan.
Hill, William J. (p. 124)
  1982 *The Three-Personed God: The Trinity as a Mystery of Salvation.* Washington, DC: Catholic University of America Press.
Hodges, Melvin L. (p. 55)
  1971 *The Indigenous Church.* Springfield: Gospel Publishing House.
Hoekendijk, J. C. (p. 68)
  1950 "The Evangelisation of Man in Modern Mass Society," *Ecumenical Review* 2, 2: 133-140.
Johnstone, P. J. (p. 33)
  1986 *Operation World*, 4th ed. Kent: STL Publications.
Julien, Tom (pp. 52, 59)
  1986 *Grace Magazine*, Special Europe Missions Issue 2, 1: 1-8.

Kane, J. Herbert (pp. 50, 66)
1986 *Trinity World Forum* 11, 2: 1-4.

Kantzer, Kenneth S. (p. 104)
1986 "Church on the Move (For the evangelical, the most exciting change in Roman Catholicism is the new freedom for the gospel)," *Christianity Today* (November 7): 16-17.

Kellar, Adolph (p. 43)
1942 *Christian Europe Today.* New York: Harper Brothers.

Koop, Allen V. (pp. 43-48, 50, 52, 55, 59, 62, 63, 64, 122, 129)
1986 *American Evangelical Missionaries in France, 1945-1975.* New York: University Press of America.

Kraemer, Hendrick (p. 89)
1958 *A Theology of the Laity.* Philadelphia: Westminster.

Kraft, Charles H. (pp. 12, 125)
1991 (1983) *Communication Theory for Christian Witness.* Maryknoll: Orbis.

Lackmann, Max (p. 116)
1963 *The Augsburg Confession and Catholic Unity.* Edited and translated by W. R. Bouman. New York: Herder & Herder.

LaCugna, Catherine Mowry (pp. 124, 130)
1991 *God For Us: The Trinity and Christian Life.* San Francisco: Harper.

Latourette, Kenneth Scott (p. 100)
1975 *A History of Christianity,* vol. 1. New York: Harper & Row.

Leclerc, Gérard (p. 77)
1986 *L'Eglise Catholique 1962-1986, Crise et Renouveau.* Paris: Editions Denoël.

Lenoir, Frédéric (p. 77)
1988 *Les Communautés Nouvelles.* Paris: Librarie Fayard.

Lindsell, Harold, ed.
1966 *The Church's Worldwide Mission.* Waco, TX: Word.

Lovelace, Richard (p. 116)
1979 *Dynamics of Spiritual Life: An Evangelical Theology of Renewal.* Downers Grove: InterVarsity.

Lowry, Charles Wesley (pp. 117, 118)
1946 *The Trinity and Christian Devotion.* London: Eyre and Spottiswoode.

Luneau, René and Paul Ladrière (p. 14)
1989 *Le Rêve de Compostelle.* Paris: Centurion.

Luzbetak, Louis J. (p. 40)
1970 *The Church and Cultures.* Techny, IL: Divine Word Publications.

MacArthur, John Jr.   (p. 100)
   1973   *The Church, the Body of Christ.* Grand Rapids: Zondervan.
Martin, Ralph
   1982   *A Crisis of Truth.* Ann Arbor: Servant Books.
Mead, Loren B.   (pp. 25, 89)
   1991   *The Once and Future Church.* Washington, DC: Alban Institute.
Mermet, Gérard   (pp. 32, 135-40)
   1995   *Francoscopie.* Paris: Larousse.
Newbigin, Lesslie   (pp. 18, 119)
   1964   *Trinitarian Faith and Today's Mission.* Richmond: John Knox.
   1987   "Can the West Be Converted?" *International Bulletin of Missionary
          Research* 11, 1: 2-7.
Ogden, Greg   (p. 89)
   1990   *The New Reformation.* Grand Rapids: Zondervan.
Olsen, Walter A.   (p. 84)
   1977   "The Dynamics of Religious Conversion in France: Research in
          Progress." Master of Theology in Missiology thesis, Fuller
          Theological Seminary School of World Mission, Pasadena, CA.
Packer, J. I.   (p. 68)
   1995   "Crosscurrents Among Evangelicals," in *Evangelicals and Catholics
          Together: Toward a Common Mission.* Charles Colson and Richard
          John Neuhaus, eds. Pp. 147-74. Dallas: Word.
Peters, George W.   (p. 27)
   1970   *Saturation Evangelism.* Grand Rapids: Zondervan.
   1981   *A Theology of Church Growth.* Grand Rapids: Zondervan.
Pohle, Joseph   (pp. 123-24, 133)
   1950   *The Divine Trinity.* St. Louis: B. Herder.
Rausch, Thomas P., S.J.   (pp. 126-27)
   1996   "Catholic-Evangelical Relations: Signs of Progress," *One in Christ*
          32, 1: 40-52.
Richard, Lucien J.   (p. 71)
   1982   *A Kenotic Christology in the Humanity of Jesus the Christ, the Compassion
          of Our God.* Washington, DC: University Press of America.
Rodgers, Thomas R.   (p. 20)
   1995   *The Panorama of the Old Testament.* Newburgh, IN: Trinity Press.
Rowdon, Harold H.   (p. 100)
   1967   "Edinburgh 1910, Evangelicals and the Ecumenical Movement"
          Vox Evangelica 5: 49-71.
Schaeffer, Francis A.   (pp. 6, 121)
   1970   *The Church at the End of the Twentieth Century.* Downers Grove:
          InterVarsity.

Schaff, Philip (p. 115)
  1958 *History of the Christian Church*, vol. 8. Grand Rapids: Eerdmans.
Schedl, Claus (pp. 19, 20)
  1972 *History of the Old Testament: The Age of the Prophets*, vol. 4. Staten Island: Alba House.
Shenk, Wilbert R. (pp. 15, 17)
  1994 "Encounters with 'Culture' Christianity," *International Bulletin of Missionary Research* 8, 1: 8-13.
Silberling, Murray (p. 130)
  1995 *Dancing for Joy*. Baltimore: Lederer Messianic Publishers.
Smeeton, Donald D. (pp. 78, 85, 89)
  1980 "Evangelical Trends in Europe, 1970-1980," *Evangelical Missions Quarterly* 16, 4: 211-16.
Snyder, Howard A.
  1975 *The Problem of Wineskins*. Downers Grove: InterVarsity.
Southern, R. W. (pp. 16-17)
  1970 *Western Society and the Church in the Middle Ages*. Grand Rapids: Eerdmans.
Spindler, Marc H. (p. 24)
  1987 "Europe's Neo-Paganism: A Perverse Inculturation," *International Bulletin of Missionary Research* 11, 1: 8-10.
Stott, John R. W. (p. 37)
  1975 *Christian Mission in the Modern World*. Downers Grove: InterVarsity.
Suenens, Leo Jozef (Cardinal) (p. 56)
  1992 "Spirit of Renewal," *The Tablet* (September 19): 1157.
Taylor, Sally A. (p. 26)
  1990 *Culture Shock France: A Guide to Customs and Etiquette*. Portland, OR: Graphic Arts Center.
Thomasius, Gottfried (p. 81)
  1965 "Christ's Person and Work," in *God and Incarnation in Mid-Nineteenth Century German Theology*. Claude Welch, ed. New York: Oxford University Press.
Throop, John R. (p. 114, 115)
  1986 "America's Catholics: Why Some Stay, Why Others Leave," *Christianity Today* (November 7): 31-33.
Torrance, Thomas F.
  1996 *The Christian Doctrine of God: One Being, Three Persons*. Edinburgh: T & T Clark.
Trueblood, David Elton (p. 92)
  1967 *The Incendiary Fellowship*. New York: Harper & Row.

Van Engen, Charles (pp. 68-69)
   1993 *God's Missionary People: Rethinking the Purpose of the Local Church.* Grand Rapids: Baker.

Vassady, Bela (p. 116)
   1965 *Christ's Church: Evangelical, Catholic and Reformed.* Grand Rapids: Eerdmans.

Ward, Maisie (p. 43)
   1949 *France Pagan? The Mission of Abbé Godin. (La France, Pays de Mission?* by Henri Godin and Yvan Daniel, translated and adapted by Maisie Ward.) New York: Sheed and Ward.

Ward, Nancy (p. 77)
   1997 "Catholic Charismatics Focusing More on Evangelism: Some Are Witnessing in the Streets Because of a New Directive from Pope John Paul II," *Charisma* 22, 10: 34-36.

Webber, Robert E. (p. 116)
   1978 *Common Roots: A Call to Evangelical Maturity.* Grand Rapids: Zondervan.

Webster, Noah (p. 13)
   1828 *An American Dictionary of the English Language.* New York: S. Converse.

Webster's New World Dictionary (p. 13)
   1970 New York: World Publishing.

Wells, David F. (pp. 100, 101, 102, 103)
   1973 *Revolution in Rome.* London: InterVarsity Christian Fellowship.

Wessels, Antoine (pp. 14, 55)
   1994 *Europe: Was It Ever Really Christian?* London: SCM.

Wilheim, Hans (pp. 63, 66)
   1986 "Chicago Consultation on Partnership in Mission in Western Europe," World Mission Associates European Project (December): 5-24.

Winter, Ralph
   1996 "What Does DeWesternization Mean?" *Mission Frontiers Bulletin Supplement* (September-October).

World Council of Churches (p. 76)
   1951 "Evangelism in France," *Ecumenical Studies.* Geneva.

World Evangelical Fellowship (pp. 38, 102, 110)
   1986 "A Contemporary Evangelical Perspective on Roman Catholicism," *Evangelical Review of Theology* 10, 4 (October-December) and 11, 1 (January-March).

Wright, Gordon (p. 35)
   1974 *France in Modern Times,* 2d ed. Chicago: Rand McNally.

Subject and Name Index

Scripture Index

Abstract

Unfamiliar Paths

The Challenge of Recognizing the
Work of Christ in Strange Clothing

–A Case Study from France–

This book explains why some missionaries are being led to reject
the missional models and many of the methodologies which are the
most widely accepted by North American evangelical missionaries
working in France. The author demonstrates that the evangelical
Protestant missionaries' witness for Christ in Western Europe is often
ineffective because their governing missional paradigm and their
ministry methods, working in conjunction, tend to project a separatist
image and isolate them from those they wish to influence for Christ.
He argues that this negative image will only be overcome as missionaries creatively and courageously develop new ways of ministering
which reflect more fully the incarnation of the God/man, Jesus Christ.

While this book focuses on France, many of its insights and argu-
ments could be applied to other post-Christendom lands. The author
suggests that we all-too-frequently err by assuming that the majority
of post-Christendom peoples have truly encountered Christ. On the
other hand, he argues that we often fail to take seriously the faith and
witness of the historical church in these lands.

In his attempt to discover how to incarnate the message of Jesus
Christ to the French, the author examines some of the characteristics
of contemporary French society, some of the needs of the dominant
Christian church in France, and the history of American evangelical
Protestant missionary activity in France since 1945. This overview
leads him to argue for the development of a missionary spirituality
based on the kenosis and an understanding of Christian unity based
on the perichoresis.